African American Women

To my parents James and Leora Peterson
and to my husband Edward Potts
whose support has been invaluable

African American Women: A Study of Will and Success

by
Elizabeth A. Peterson

McFarland & Company, Inc., Publishers
Jefferson, North Carolina, and London

Acknowledgments. I would like to acknowledge and thank those who have been so supportive of me in my efforts on this book. First, I would like to thank all the strong, African American women I interviewed. Sisters, you invited me into your homes and your offices; sometimes we met in restaurants to chat over coffee. Wherever we met, you opened your hearts up to me. Your stories and insights into your lives provided the meat of this study. I thank you.

I also would like to thank Phyllis Cunningham. Her energy and enthusiasm are contagious. To Sherman Stanage I am deeply grateful, for he assured me when I was in doubt that I really do understand what phenomenology is. Tom Heaney inspired me to think more critically and always provided clear and useful criticism. Patricia Harbour served as a special reader and gave me valuable criticism from a Black female perspective. Thank you. I would be remiss if I didn't mention Paul Ilsley, who was that rare thing – both a boss and a friend.

My special thanks to all my "girlfriends" who have been my sounding boards, especially to Vera, Verdonna, Michele, and Marcheta, who have at one time or another heard all my ideas. Many thanks to my dear friend Chester; I couldn't have done it without him. He challenged every word I wrote; but not only that, he allowed me to borrow, indefinitely, every book in his marvelous collection.

Most of all, I thank my family and thank God for giving me the best mother, father, sister, and brothers in the world. They never doubted that I could do this. I give my final and special thanks to my mother, Leora Elizabeth Peterson. She is the strong-willed, African American woman whom I have always strived to imitate. She taught me to believe in myself and know that I was a special person. She believed in my dream and made it her own.

British Library Cataloguing-in-Publication data are available

Library of Congress Cataloguing-in-Publication Data

Peterson, Elizabeth A., 1956–
    African American women : a study of will and success / by
Elizabeth A. Peterson.
        p. cm.
    Includes bibliographical references and index.
    ISBN 0-89950-730-1 (sewn softcover : 55# alk. paper) ∞
    1. Afro-American women.   2. Will.   3. American literature – Afro-
American authors – History and criticism.   4. American literature –
Women authors – History and criticism.   5. Will in literature.
I. Title.
E185.86.P5   1992
305.48'896073 – dc20   92-54088
                                                                CIP

Manufactured in the United States of America

McFarland & Company, Inc., Publishers
  Box 611, Jefferson, North Carolina 28640

Table of Contents

Introduction

Black women whose ancestors were brought to the United States beginning in 1619 have lived through conditions of cruelties so horrible, so bizarre, the women had to re-invent themselves. They had to find safety and sanctity inside themselves or they would not have been able to tolerate those tortuous lives. They had to learn to be self-forgiving quickly, for often their exterior exploits were at odds with their interior beliefs. Still they had to survive as wholly and healthily as possible in an infectious and sick climate.

—Maya Angelou[1]

This passage, taken from Brian Lanker's book, *I Dream a World,* sums up what is meant by self-will. It is the ability to reinvent oneself, to transcend the forces that would act upon humanity and destroy it, to be self-caused.

The African American woman has struggled against innumerable odds since slavery. With social and economic deprivation, sexism, and racism providing constant blocks, it is remarkable that history is so full of rich examples of Black women who have defied the odds. Black history can point to many examples of great determination and will in African American women. Women like Harriet Tubman, Mary McCleod-Bethune, and Rosa Parks devoted their lives to the struggle for freedom and justice, and changed American history. They were slaves or daughters of slaves, poor, and constantly confronted with sexism and racism. They, like many of their lesser-known sisters, took for granted that, for them, life was going to be "no crystal stair."[2] As mothers, daughters, laborers, teachers and keepers of the faith, African American women have made great contributions to their communities and the world.

Yet we cannot take the will or inner strength of Black women for granted. This is especially true considering the many problems now facing the Black community. Twenty years after the Civil Rights Move-

1

ment, the Black community is still far behind in the fight for social equality and justice. Black women and children are still among the poorest in the nation. Unemployment, violence, and drugs seem to be sapping the vitality out of Black people, both male and female.

It is important to search for a deeper understanding of the strong will of the Black woman. How have Black women in the past had the courage to confront their conditions and overcome the barriers to their greatness? What kinds of experiences and influences did they have that allowed them to make an impact on history?

Adult educators today can benefit from a better understanding of the development of a strong human will in African American women. Too many Black youths and young adults are abandoning our nation's schools. Many young adults are apathetic and drained of will rather than resolved to resist the forces of oppression and poverty. As some of these women return to school and enter adult education programs, it is important that we use the opportunity to revive their will.

I intend this book to give hope to the countless Black women who are still struggling and who are in small ways daily reinventing themselves. I offer these investigations to assist those adult educators who believe that the purpose of education is not only to form the individual, but to transform as well. It will also, I hope, be a worthy addition to a debate that has gone on for centuries – the debate over the existence and the nature of the human will.

In this book, the terms "African American" and "Black" will be used interchangeably to denote people of African heritage. Recently, there has been a shift in terminology, and "African American" is now more frequently used. I personally prefer the term "Black." I feel that color has been the issue in the practices of racial discrimination and injustice. Using the term "Black" serves as a constant reminder that we still must confront the issue of racism.

Chapter 1 briefly discusses the concept of will as it is commonly understood today. The debate over the nature of the human will has been never-ending. The concept has been approached from many perspectives, such as theological, philosophical, and psychological. The background of each of these debates will be presented in brief terms.

In Chapter 2 a brief history of phenomenology will be presented, followed by an explanation of the "steps" involved in a phenomenological inquiry. Reasons will be offered for the use of the approach in this book. The chapter will conclude by retracing the debate in Chapter 1, applying the steps of phenomenology and beginning to trace the development of will from a Black perspective.

Chapter 3 moves from a general understanding of self-will to more specific discussion about the will of Black women. This chapter consists of three distinct sections.

Themes of will abound in the literature of Black female authors. The chapter will first search for themes of will found in the novels of three very prominent authors: Zora Neale Hurston, Alice Walker, and Toni Morrison.

The life of Zora Neale Hurston, an anthropologist, novelist, and creative force of the Harlem Renaissance, will be the focus in the second section of Chapter 3. Hurston's unique gifts and vital spirit were of great influence to Black female authors who followed her, including Alice Walker. Section 3 of this chapter will search for themes of self-will in the autobiographical writings of Maya Angelous, a Black woman whose struggle has been brilliantly described in her award-winning books. By examining the themes of self-will in the writings of these authors, I hope to establish some essential structures for the development of will in Black women.

Chapter 4 investigates the themes and essential structures revealed in the previous chapter. Through personal interviews, contemporary African American women speak for themselves to tell the stories of their life experiences, struggles, and successes. New themes and essential structures may emerge and the old themes may be tested and challenged.

The material for Chapter 4 came from life stories collected from 30 Black women, ages 25 to 95. A scientific formula was not used in obtaining names. I shared my research interests with friends and associates and asked for lists of women who were considered strong role models, leaders in the community, or who, in other ways, exemplified the quality of strong will and self-determination. I received many lists of names and sent out over one hundred letters to women. I conducted all of the interviews between March and August of 1990.

From the 30 interviews, I selected 15 to include in the study. All names of interviewees used in this book have been changed to protect their identity. I eliminated all of the interviews of women who were under 30 years of age. I found that most of these younger women were still very uncertain about themselves and their goals. These interviews were generally much weaker than those who were 30 and older. For example, several of the younger women felt that they were successful only because they had "good luck." These women could not verbalize the events that led up to their present success, except that they were good at following directions and worked very hard. In one instance, a young woman revealed that she was really overwhelmed by her position. The final 15 interviews were with women who most exemplified great courage and will; that is, they each had overcome significant obstacles: poverty, abuse, racism, or a life crisis. They confronted these obstacles and moved on with their lives.

The women not only varied in age, they also varied in educational attainment and socioeconomic status. Two of the women I interviewed had obtained a GED, six had completed high school and had a few years of college, three were college graduates, and four had completed advanced degrees. The women have various occupations. One woman is a housewife; one is employed as a domestic and one is a retired domestic. There is a computer analyst, four women have supervisory responsibilities at the United States Post Office, and two women are employed as social workers. There is one community organizer, one elementary school teacher, an attorney, an artist and entrepreneur, and a nun who is also an assistant professor at the Catholic seminary.

Chapter 5 offers an African American interpretation of self-will. In this chapter the relationship between the development of the strong will and the success of Black women is explored. This chapter also offers implications for professionals in adult education.

Many Black women are participants in adult education and literacy programs across the nation. They have been served by practices based on generic adult learning theories. This study will suggest how adult education theory, practice, and research can be enriched by a better understanding of the Black perspective as well as provide directions for future research.

Chapter 1

The Human Will

Is not this corporeal figure apparent to all whose senses are
perfect? Why then speaks it not the same to all? Animals small
and great see it, but they cannot ask it: because no reason is
set over their senses to judge on what they report. But men
can ask, so the invisible things of God are clearly seen, being
understood by the things that are made....

— St. Augustine[3]

The debate about the nature of the human will has continued unresolved
for centuries. While the Western debate is not particularly relevant to
the African American understanding, it has served and continues to
serve as the legitimate framework for all serious discussion. Philosophers, theologians and psychologists have participated in this debate.
They have agreed and disagreed, yet have still not reconciled whether
free will exists at all. So many questions remain unanswered, though the
greatest of minds have pondered them. Is there a human will? From
where does it come? Is it divine? Why do some seem to have more will
than others? Are will and motivation synonymous? Are will and power
synonymous? Is there a general lack of will today? These are just a few
of the questions, but they do suggest the intensity of the argument. It is
important to note these questions are still relevant today.

To enter the debate on the nature of the human will, it is helpful to
first trace the history of the debate. There are two questions that preface
any discussion of the existence of will. The *first* is the question of causality. What causes any event to happen, or do things happen merely by
chance? Can human beings change the course of events, or are our lives
predetermined? The *second* question is, What is the nature of freedom?
Are we as humans free to exercise our wills? Can we intervene to change
the course of events? If so, at what point can we intervene? Can humans
be free to exercise their will and remain free, or does one person's

freedom lead to another's bondage? These are a few of the questions which become relevant.

Will and Cause

It is commonly understood by those who believe in the existence of the human will that human beings are unique creatures within the universe. Human beings can operate beyond the capacity of all the "lower" animals: We can exert our will. "Among the billions of things that move, only man moves to carry out his will."[4] Human beings make decisions that affect themselves and all other creatures around them. Humans can decide events and change the world. We believe that by our will we determine our being and becoming. However, do we really? Do we really operate freely to decide what will be or do we really only react and act within the conditions in which we find ourselves? Can we pinpoint causes for anything in existence? A discussion of the nature of causality and determinism is necessary to build a foundation for an argument about will.

What Is Causality?

Today we seem to take the meaning of the word "cause" for granted in our daily speech. We use the word "because" to answer almost every "why" question without realizing we are making an assumption that events can be caused. In fact this has been a question that has been debated for many years.

The meaning of the word "cause" has changed over the centuries. When we speak of causes today, most of the time we mean reasons. We refer to the "how" of events – how they happened and what took place. We call these the reasons or the causes of an event. Often we list the causes as a series of actions or movements that prompted events.

In Greek, however, there was a different meaning attached to the word cause. With the notion of cause, there also existed the notion of responsibility. Rather than describe how events happened, the ancient scholars looked for whatever could be assigned responsibility for the event.[5] This differs greatly from our present understanding. Would we, for example, always hold the sun responsible for melting snow? Is the rain always responsible for the river?

According to Aristotle, there are four causes which can explain anything in our experience. Combinations of these causes can be used to explain any event, and it is up to us to offer what explanation we can.

The first cause is the material cause. This accounts for the occurrence of a phenomenon by the substances of which it is made. For example, we know fire to be heat energy. It is also combustion. Fire is not cool and it is not wet, so water cannot be a fire. Only fire has the characteristics of exploding heat. Therefore, we know fire by its material cause.

The efficient cause is the second form of cause. A fire is a fire because someone or some chain of events started the fire. A lit match or the arsonist could be the efficient cause. Later (in the sixteenth century, especially), the efficient cause became the most frequently used meaning in common discourse on causality.

Another cause is what Aristotle termed the formal cause. Things and events take on patterns that we as humans recognize and name. A fire is a fire because we have the concept of fire within our experience. We differentiate between things and events because of their unique patterns. Particular fires may stand out in our memory, and we will be able to name them and the events that led up to them.

The fourth cause is one which Aristotle called the final cause. This cause is based on the appearance that some aspects of nature seemed to have. Nature seemed to have some predetermined goal or purpose. It also can be considered synonymous with the word reason. It is the purpose or intention for which an object or event has being. We could then say, to use the fire example again, that the final cause or reason for the discovery of fire was that humans needed the warmth it provided. Thus, that which already existed in nature took on a new meaning when it was captured, contained, and used for the comforts of human beings. This is the final cause.[6]

Aristotle did not intend that we limit the number of causes used to describe events of nature. We should look for the possibility of all four causes in every event so that we might have a richer account of each event we experience. We have, however, limited ourselves. In the human realm, and especially through the influence of the earlier behaviorists following B. F. Skinner, most often we look for the chain reaction or the stimulus-response. This is but one cause however – the efficient cause. Many modern philosophers have rejected this notion of cause altogether saying that true causal relationships cannot be established and that what we mean by cause is merely statistical probability.[7]

Robin G. Collinwood, for example, reopened Aristotle's debate and, in *An Essay on Metaphysics*, outlined three senses of causation.[8] He characterizes Sense I causation as the free and deliberate act of a conscious and responsible agent. When we speak of a person or event "causing" an act, we really are suggesting that a motive has been provided for the act. Two elements make up a cause of this nature, a *causa quod* or an efficient cause and a *causa ut* or final cause. The *causa quod* is a situation or believed state of things existing; the *causa ut* is a purpose or state of things to be caused, the intention.

In this sense, if we speak of a person who is self-caused, we are referring to a person who acts without the persuasion of another. Here the *causa quod* is the same as the *causa ut*.

Sense II of Collingwood's theory comes from practical science and refers to an event or state of things that human power can either produce or prevent.[9] For example, medical researchers work to find the "cause" of a disease. Why? To enable them to intervene and prevent the disease from developing or spreading. In Sense II, "cause" refers to a person concerned with an opinion about the event's cause such that the event may be produced or prevented upon demand. A disease can be caused by any number of variables, but the researcher is concerned only about the point where he or she can intervene. That is the most relevant cause.

Collingwood describes Sense III of cause as having two conditions. The first condition is that cause exists whether humans want it to exist or not. Nothing or no one can either produce or prevent it. The second condition is that the cause exists by producing its effect, no matter what else exists or does not exist. There are no *conditiones sine quibus non*. The cause leads to its effect by itself, unconditionally.[10]

This sense of cause is closely linked to theoretical physical science. It implies that in nature there are events over which no human has control. It is this sense of cause that is often linked with God. If we have no human control over these events, then they must be controlled by a force more powerful than any human force.

Collingwood concludes by saying that belief in causation is based on a conception of God as a semi-anthropomorphic being. His belief implies that God has a power not belonging to man – the power of creating instruments of His will that are themselves possessed of will.[11]

We should not be limited by language that suggests that cause is only a relationship as in "A causes B." Neither Aristotle nor Collingwood found it to be that simple. We can, however, recognize that human intervention is possible. If we find the point where we can intervene, does it really matter if it is or is not a real cause? Perhaps, at the point of human intervention, we have not grasped the real cause, or there may be many other causes. But is this grasp essential, or is it more important that we find a point of action where we can exert our will?

We clearly believe that we have the knowledge that we can act and change events. This belief, coupled with Aristotle's concept that we exist to move toward a goal or purpose, must be presupposed for any other discussion of will to be coherent and useful in human affairs. For it is through acting based on our knowledge of being, and our belief that our lives have purpose that we find freedom.

Absolute Freedom and the Will

We have come to think of freedom as meaning unrestricted, unbound, to be able to act without constraints. In fact, however, none of us is free in this sense. We do not have absolute freedom, for we have not returned to a state of nature as defined by English philosopher Thomas Hobbes, but relinquish our freedom in the name of common security and happiness. As citizens in a "free" country, we are bound by the laws of the land. As members of families and communities, we are restricted (both constrained and restrained) by the norms, mores, customs, and beliefs that identify us as members of that family or community. If we consider that we never have absolute freedom, then we realize that "freedom is always a matter of more or less, and that what we are concerned with in discussions of freedom is the type and extent of limitation put upon our behavior. The more limitations, the less freedom."[12]

How we understand freedom and free choice affects how we understand free will and self-determination. According to Silvano Arieti, we never have complete freedom, and it is illusory to think so.

> The issue is not between determinism and free choice, but relative determinism and relative free choice. The extent of this relative free choice depends on health or disease, intelligence, amount of knowledge, state of organism, environmental opportunities, social factors, emotional conditions, and importantly the state of consciousness of many of our ideas and attitudes.[13]

Therefore, those with more favorable life conditions should be more able to exercise their will. Those who are "free" can become more "free." By acting within our limitations, we can obtain more of this relative freedom for it is within our nature to strive to overcome those forces that limit us.

> Striving for freedom is an unceasing attempt to overcome the conditions of physicochemistry, biology, psychology, and society that affect

human life. To the extent that man succeeds in transcending these conditions he becomes self-caused ... this self-causation is only a thin margin of a totality in which the majority is ruled deterministically ... but this thin margin is important enough to change the world.[14]

Maxine Greene writes that one way we can conceive of freedom is that it is the "ability to alter situations by reinterpreting them and, by so doing, seeing oneself as a person in a new perspective. Once this happens, there are new beginnings, new actions to undertake in the world."[15]

It is this continual striving for freedom in an attempt to transcend the limitations of racism, sexism, and substandard economic conditions, not to mention the limitations of laws, culture, and tradition, which makes the Black woman a remarkable study of will. Black women have been a pivotal force of their homes and communitites. They have made a great impact on this nation on issues from slavery to freedom, while continuing to strive for personal dignity and recognition.

This leads the discussion back to the nature of the human will. To some extent, the Black woman is self-caused; she exists and succeeds precisely because she wills it. The strong Black woman moves through action to that final cause or purpose for which she is. The whole story of the Black experience in America can never be known. There are too many individual voices which have not been heard. However, adult educators can find a new meaning to their work by investigating and presenting their findings to larger publics.

> ...recall Blacks suffering discrimination all the way, challenging, forever challenging "the wall." We who are in education cannot know, cannot truly know how it was, how it is. But we can attend to some of the voices, some of the stories. And as we do so, our perspectives on the meanings of freedom and the possibility of freedom in this country may particularize and expand.[16]

Both the concept of causality and the concept of freedom serve as a foundation for a discussion of the free human will. The following sections will examine the evolution of thought relating to the human will in Western theology, philosophy, and psychology.

A Theological Debate

The debate concerning free human will in Western theology began out of an attempt to assign a purpose to nature. This debate began long before

Judeo-Christianity or Islam. Even in the mythology of the ancient Greeks and Romans, "gods" possessing superior intelligence were given credit for that which no person could take credit. With the coming of Judaism and Christianity, perfection – the perfection of the universe – was considered a product of God. At this point, "science" and "theology" were in general accord. The universe had rational and reliable laws that governed it, and this rationality and reliability came from God.

The perfection of the universe and the order of nature were even used to prove the existence of God before creation. St. Anselm reinterpreted Aristotle's First or Final cause as the Judeo-Christian God. Citing Aristotle's use of efficient cause (every "effect" has a "cause"), Anselm sought to prove God's existence by tracing back all the cause and effect events. Anselm concluded that two outcomes were possible – an eternal regression of cause and effect events or a beginning, a "First Cause."[17] Therefore, Anselm believed that God put the order in the universe.

In Anselm's analogy, the work of God is much like the artistic expression of an artisan. God created something from nothing, as was His intention. The artisan creates from the image in his mind. However, Anselm goes on to say that even this analogy is incomplete. Humans are unable to create from nothing. Since the exact image that the artisan is creating from exists only in his mind, the creation must come from the memory of known physical objects.[18] Human beings can only build from that which already exists in nature. This limitation was seen as the major difference in God's will and human will.

Christian traditions dictate that God is the supreme law or creator. The extent that humans have been given authority to exercise their individual will is where the debate begins.

The Scripture on Free Will

If one uses the Bible as the basis for an argument on free will, there are many passages that establish God as the creator of men and women. One may also determine that God wishes to establish a relationship that allows for human choice. In Genesis 1:26–30, God makes man and woman in His own image. "So God created human beings making them like himself. He created them male and female, blessed them, and said, 'Have many children, so that your descendants will live all over the earth and bring it under their control.'"[19]

God, therefore, created humans to be corulers of a sort according to this passage. In Genesis 2, there is a second story of creation. This time

God creates man and woman and places them in the Garden of Eden. As in the first creation story, they are created like God, except in the second story humans lack wisdom or the knowledge of good and evil. God forbids Adam and Eve to eat the fruit of the tree that will give them this knowledge, but they exercise free will and disobey God. Why? Because the serpent promises Eve that if she eats from the tree, she will become like God in all ways.[20] She will have wisdom. So according to this passage, human beings first exercise their will and disobey God to be like God!

In Genesis 22, we have Abraham, an old man when Sarah bears him a long-awaited son. God commands Abraham to give up this beloved son as a sacrifice. Abraham has a choice. He chooses to obey God, and by so doing seals his covenant with God and becomes the father of his people.[21]

Perhaps the most extraordinary account of the exercise of free will, however, comes from the book of Jonah. In this story, Jonah is commanded by God to go to Ninevah, speak out against the evil there, and warn of God's wrath. Jonah has a choice. He decides to do none of what God commanded and instead tries to run from God. Jonah, in turn, is swallowed into the stomach of a whale. God allowed Jonah to choose, but God also was able to punish Jonah.

In the third chapter of Jonah, we find Jonah obeying the Lord and fulfilling his destiny as a prophet to the people. Jonah was spared, and Ninevah was spared.

Even in the New Testament of the Bible the ability of humans to make free choices is mentioned. In Matthew 7:21-23 and also in Luke 13:25-27, Jesus suggests that people are free to choose salvation. Those who recognize the Lord and do what they should do will find recognition by the Lord. Those who do not know the Lord will not be known to God.

More Theological Interpretations

The problem therefore is not one of content, but one of interpretation. Even among Western theologians who believe wholeheartedly in free will, there has been little agreement on how free will actually works. How does God retain a relationship of authority if human beings have the right to act of their own will?

St. Paul proposed the "deterministic thesis" that stated that there was a period when humans were free, but this was lost with original sin. God, however, determined before the world was created that some would be saved through grace. A person who wanted to reassure himself and others of his or her salvation would behave in a righteous manner.[22] St. Augustine of Hippo expanded St. Paul's "deterministic thesis" by equating the free will of humans with evil. In his *Confessions,* he wrote:

> And I strained to perceive what I now heard, that free will was the cause of our doing ill, and Thy just judgment of our suffering ill. But I was not able clearly to discern it. So then endeavouring to draw my soul's vision out of that deep pit, I was again plunged therein, and endeavouring often, I was plunged back often. But this raised me a little into Thy light, that I knew as well that I had a will, as that I lived: when then I did will or nill any thing, I was most sure that no other than myself did will and nill: and I all but saw that there was the cause of my sin. But what I did against my will, I saw that I suffered rather than did, and I judged not to be my fault, but my punishment; whereby however, holding Thee to be just, I speedily confessed myself to be not unjustly punished.[23]

Augustine not only believed that freedom was lost because of original sin, he believed that the will to do evil was gained. Human will was the cause of human suffering and it was only through denying ourselves and our evil nature and seeking to do God's will, which is always good, that we as humans can be good.

St. Thomas Aquinas believed that though human will does reflect causality, this remains secondary to the causality of God. Evil arises out of ignorance or lack of reason as misplaced good. Human beings do not have the superior knowledge of God. If we did and knew all the ramifications for our actions, we would avoid errors in reasoning and our resulting behavior would be that which God had predetermined for us.[24] In other words, if we knew what God knows about us and about our behavior in the light of what is good and what is evil, we would naturally opt for good.

Martin Luther bitterly argued with Erasmus about the nature of free will. Luther contended that all human action was predetermined by God. Will then is seen as an action directed toward God. Erasmus was more of a humanist. He argued that human beings could reject grace and freely determine their destiny.[25]

While all of the theological interpretations presented are sound and rational, they do not necessarily reflect human action in an ever changing world.

Contemporary Interpretations of Free Will

The debate continues among contemporary Western theologians about the nature of free will and the relationship between God as creator, the supreme will, and humans as free creative agents. Theologians differ in outlook depending upon whether they are Protestant or Catholic, fundamentalist, reformed, or professing a theology of liberation.

One view is that while humans do have free will, it is a gift from God. It is borne out of God's free self-manifestation and sharing. It is a reward for being an image and likeness of God in the realm of creative activity.[26]

But human beings in full exercise of their wills have the option of saying "no" to God. When a person does this, she or he does not lose the power to exercise free will but, by being disconnected from God – the creative force – a person will eventually lose the capability to love and do good. To be connected is important for the exercise of good will, that is, the power to be creative rather than destructive.

Another view is that "God instead of being at an ominous, transcendent distance is close in incomprehensible goodness . . . man does not have to protect his freedom. God's rule and man's activity are not mutually exclusive."[27]

In this view, God and humans work together in a spirit of cooperation. God in his love for us can allow us to exercise our will, even if that will sends us astray, but God is also a loving father, willing to welcome us upon our return.

Finally, there are those who believe that to speak of will is much the same as speaking of "spirits" or "powers." It is too vague. They prefer to speak of "willing" as a verb rather than the noun "will." Willing is seen as observable, empirically perceptible. It is the deliberate decision for a particular orientation of action.[28]

The next step in understanding the development of the current discussion of human will is to follow the progression of the debate, this time from the perspective of philosophy.

A Philosophical Debate

One does not have to believe in God, however, to believe in a free human will. Although early Western philosophical thought on the topic somewhat parallels the thought of the theologians, there are differences. Later philosophers, Nietzsche in particular, while believing in human will, did not believe in God. Nietzsche denounced religious belief and moral values based on religious principles and predicted a total collapse of traditional value systems. "Nihilism" would result in the assent of the human will to power and the formation of new value systems.[29]

At the beginning of this chapter, Aristotle and the concept of causality as a foundation for the concept of will were discussed. The fact is that the Greeks lacked a notion of will at that time. Aristotle equates the decision to do something with the actual action (*De Motu Animalium* 701 a21) and says nothing more than that once we decide to do something, then "all at once and quickly" we act. So there are only decisions and actions with no mental processes between which enhance or impede the action.

Descartes was the next most important Western philosopher to contribute to the theory of will. For Descartes, we could only say that something exists if we have a clear and distinct idea of it. We have no clear and distinct idea of what separates soul and body; or thought and action. We have even less of an idea about how these things happen to come together. Yet, according to Descartes, we do know that there is a connection. We perceive the connection even though the nature is unclear and indistinct. This inexplicable connection is the "will." In this, we must have faith, and faith is the exception to general rules of evidence. Faith is not an act of the intellect, but of the will which, disposed by God's revelation, can assent even without evidence.[30]

Locke in many ways remained true to this position, but called the "will" the power by which we move from thought to action. The mind directs the will; the will creates a volition which acts as a directive, a "willingness," and finally the action occurs.

Kant believed that everything in nature worked according to the laws of nature, but only humans (as they are rational beings) could act out of understanding of the laws. This capacity is the will. Since reason is required to decide actions from laws, will is nothing more than practical reason.

When we will, therefore, what we are doing is deciding action from the universal laws as we understand them. When we understand a law, gravity, for example, and act according to our understanding, in designing an airplane, let's say, then we are willing. When we have no choice but to act according to the law, such as falling down the stairs, we are not willing.

Kant believed this to be true also of moral laws that he felt were as universal as physical laws. If we understand the principles of the laws and act accordingly, then we are exercising our will. If we act according to law only because the law is imposed on us, then we are not exercising will. We are not free.

When we consider the views of other thinkers, it is evident that the argument has not advanced very far. William James accepted will as a metaphysical question, not one that could be answered with a clear definition. He looked instead for a scientific theory of action. The will is that which keeps the action within the consciousness, and the real strain of willing is the effort to keep the consciousness clear and the attention focussed. Attention or intention becomes the seat of the will.[31]

James asserts that it is the point of momentary lapse in consciousness when the original thought or idea exerts effect. This produces the volition, and the act occurs. There is no decision making in the process. He gives the following example of how one comes to exert one's will:

> We know what it is to get out of bed on a freezing morning in a room without a fire and how the very vital principle within us protests against the ordeal. Probably most persons have lain on certain mornings for an hour at a time unable to brace themselves to the resolve. We think how late we shall be, how the duties of the day will suffer; we say, "I must get up, this is ignominious," and so on. But still the warm couch feels too delicious, and the cold outside too cruel, and resolution faints away and postpones itself again and again just as it seemed on the verge of the decisive act. Now how do we ever get up under such circumstances? If I may generalize from my own experience, we more often than not get up without any struggle or decision at all. We suddenly find that we have got up. A fortunate lapse of consciousness occurs; we forget both the warmth and the cold; we fall into some revery connected with the day's life, in the course of which the idea flashes across us, "Hollo! I must lie here no longer" – an idea which at that lucky instant awakens no contradictory or paralyzing suggestions, and consequently produces immediately its appropriate motor effects. It was our acute consciousness of both the warmth and the cold during the period of struggle which paralyzed our activity.[32]

Of course, James offers us no definitive analysis. Something has to happen between the point of struggle and the point where we find ourselves acting. We all have found ourselves in a situation when a split second decision must be made and then we can act. But how? The key, perhaps, is that in the "lapse of consciousness" that James describes, there is the point where some different thought process is going on. According to James, we "fall into a revery connected with the day's life."

Falling into reverie is significant. Perhaps it is not connected with decision making at all, but with a different vision. Perhaps in the vision we see the act as already being completed, and our bodies just move to keep up with the vision. James then believes that what we really do when we exert our will is to fill our minds with an idea that would ordinarily slip away. We give mental consent to a fact. "The fact always appears to us by its idea becoming victorious over internal and external difficulties, banishing contradictory ideas and remaining in stable possession of the mind."[33]

So we are still left with will being the point that lies somewhere between the thought and the action. Nothing is clear even yet except that will is the meeting point of mind and body; the spiritual and the physical; and the soul and the flesh. Descartes said that the principal problem in defining the will is that one cannot define what is extended (the body) in the terms of the unextended (the mind). At this point, let's return to a very different perspective of will.

It is not necessary to believe in God, the soul, the spirit, or in the supernatural to believe in the human will. This view leads to a discussion of Friedrich Nietzsche and the relationship between power and the human will.

> All the beauty and sublimity we have bestowed upon real and imaginary things I will reclaim as the property and product of man: as his fairest apology. Man as poet, as thinker, as God, as love, as power: with what regal liberality he has lavished gifts upon things so as to impoverish himself and make himself feel wretched! His most unselfish act hitherto has been to admire and worship and to know how to conceal from himself that it was he who created what he admired.[34]

This selection from *The Will to Power* sums up Nietzsche's view of how far humankind had come. People had become impoverished caricatures of what they could be and of what they should be. This impoverishment occurred because humans turned over their wills to God and refused to admit their own natures. They would not take credit for the good that existed in the world, nor would they accept the evil and, for that reason, humans were weak.

Nietzsche predicted the complete destruction of present value systems (nihilism) and pointed to prevailing conditions as signs of nihilism's certainty. Nietzsche was an atheist. He went beyond typical disbelief and proclaimed that "God is dead.... And we have killed him." To understand the message of Nietzsche, it is necessary to in some way understand what led him to such a view of God and religion. Then we can understand what his particular message is in relation to the human will.

Nietzsche was born in 1844 in Germany. He was born in a time when traditional theology and religion was challenged as it had never been. In 1859, Charles Darwin published *On the Origin of Species*, an event

which rocked the religious community. Debates on evolution versus creation, and God versus science raged. This debate influenced the young
Nietzsche (a pastor's son who up to that time had accepted traditional
Christian thought). He showed early genius; and when he left for the
university, his life changed. He became an atheist. He could not reconcile
the teachings he found in the Bible with what seemed to be fact, and he
grew more depressed. It was during that time that Nietzsche became
greatly influenced by another philosopher, Arthur Schopenhauer. Schopenhauer, a pessimist, had written a book called *The World as Will and
Idea*. Nietzsche read it, and after that was not only an atheist, but anti–
Christian.

Schopenhauer argued (as a response against Kant) that things in
themselves do not exist. There are only ideas of things. All things are
only appearances beyond which human knowledge and science do not ex-
tend. We know "appearances," "phenomena," not "things in themselves,
still less an Absolute, least of all God."[35]

Schopenhauer went on to say that man can only experience himself
in two ways: outwardly as object of the idea and inwardly as expression
of will.

The meaning of will here is very distinct. Schopenhaur felt that the
innermost drive of all human beings is the will to live. "The urge to live,
this primordial will, that appears in all appearances: the world of the idea
exists as will making its appearance. The world is 'in its whole nature
through and through will, and at the same time through and through
idea.' "[36]

The world is, therefore, because we will it to be. In every act, we pro-
claim our own will to live. This will is the essence of all the universe and
is the "thing in itself." For Schopenhauer, the force behind all existence
was not God, but the will to live. Life's pains and disappointments were
all a result of the will to live. It was only through recognition of the pain
and suffering, the relinquishing of the will, and the discovery of true compassion that humans could redeem themselves, could enter into unity
with the "All in One."[37]

This struggle of life and death impressed Nietzsche, but he went
even further in his theory. Nietzsche believed in the will as power. He did
not buy into any notion of relinquishing will, he believed in acknowledging the will. For Nietzsche, the primordial drive was not the "will to live"
but the "will to power." Humans had been duped into giving up their
power, but this was unnatural. As people began to realize their mistake,
nihilism would be the result. The biggest deceiver had been Christianity.
By using "spiritual enlightenment," men with strong wills were able to

suppress and make weak the wills of the masses.[38] Nietzsche offers parallels between sickliness and weakness. "Just as health and sickness are not essentially different, there is no difference between evil and good, both are exaggerations . . . weakness is the negation of life."[39]

Nietzsche says repeatedly that weakness of the will is a result of nihilism, but he also says that nihilism is a result of the weakness of will. This is the somewhat ambiguous indictment that makes Nietzsche a little hard to take. It would be wrong, however, to dismiss all that he says as the ramblings of a madman. One thing is clear – Nietzsche felt there was a weakening in the spirit of human beings. He linked that weakening to religions, especially Christianity, because in the context of religion humans put the responsibility for life outside themselves. This was a mistake. Human beings should take what they could for themselves. The human will is to be powerful, to be in control, to be creative. "Higher man is distinguished from lower man by his fearlessness and readiness to challenge misfortune . . . physiological fatigue, feebleness of will are signs of degeneration. Abundant strength wants to create, suffer, go under. . . ."[40]

The argument about the nature of the human will goes on. The picture is still cloudy even after the writings of the most renowned theologians and philosophers are consulted. I will move on to psychology to see if the view there presents a clearer picture.

A Debate in Psychology

From the perspective of behavioral psychology, the answer is simple: will does not exist. Behaviorists dating back to John Watson, the founder of the school of objective psychology, find nothing to suggest that will is a factor at all in human behavior. Human action is part of a stimulus-response chain. Nature, for the behaviorist, is ordered in this way and human beings as part of nature are no different. Human beings are therefore conditioned to respond to stimuli. The human being can be thought of as "an assembled organic machine ready to run."[41]

B. F. Skinner is another behaviorist who had little use for the concept of human will. In Skinner's view, "will plays no role in our life; there is no such thing as the autonomous man."[42]

For these behavioral psychologists, every human behavior can be traced back to a cause and effect relationship. "Behavior is responsivity which is itself the 'effect' of an antecedent 'cause'. . . . But in no instance is there 'that for the sake of which' prediction directing behavior in an intentional or purposive fashion."[43]

With Sigmund Freud and the coming of psychoanalysis, the notion of will is still seen as an illusion. This is in part due to the way will was defined and treated in Victorian Europe. Will was a repressor and having "willpower" was defined as having the capacity to deny oneself. It was not viewed as a powerful, creative force.

According to Freud, will gets in the way of action, true expression, and choice by putting repression and resistance in the forefront. Will was replaced by id, superego, and the external world; and when seeking the force and motive of human activity, Freud looked to the "vicissitudes of instincts" and the "fact of the repressed libido"[44] instead of will.

There are others in the field who not only believe there is a human will, they also believe that humans can improve their will. Dr. Robert Assagioli, in *The Act of Will*, states that "will is closely linked with the 'Self'. It can change a person's self-awareness and one's whole attitude toward oneself, other people, and the world."[45] He outlines three phases in the establishment of will: (1) recognition that will exists, (2) realization of having a will, and (3) being a will.[46] He feels that the discovery of will usually takes place in a moment of revelation. Often this occurs at a crisis point, but also can happen during periods of silence and meditation. During these periods, our inner voices can speak and we can be receptive to them.

The will has a directive and regulatory function as well. The will balances life in that it allows us to use all our energies constructively. There is an aspect of temporality in the will; the present is sacrificed for the sake of the future.[47] This is not, however, repression; it is discipline.

Assagioli gives four dimensions of the human will: the strong will, the skillfull will, the good will, and the transpersonal will.[48] All of these dimensions should be developed for the person to make the greatest use of their will. A person who does not develop each may find that the will can be used poorly, for destruction rather than creation.

> In each of us there are potentially all the elements and qualities of the human being, the germs of all virtues and vices. In each of us there is the potential criminal and the potential saint or hero. It is a question of different development, valuation choice, control, and expression.[95]

As every person is in a constant state of development, the will can be strengthened. "The desire or willingness to push on and challenge life comes from the experiences we have and how we interpret them."[50] "Willing" is a process, with stages, that can be pinpointed and strengthened if need be. Assagioli outlines the stages of willing as: (1) the purpose, aim, or goal based on evaluation, motivation, and intention; (2) deliberation; (3) choice and decision; (4) affirmation; (5) planning and working out; and (6) direction of execution.

The principal cause of failure in completing an act of will, according to Assagioli, is that people have difficulty carrying out one or another specific stage.[51] For example, many people set goals or make resolutions, but never see them out. Establishing the aim or the goal is only the first step, while willing has several phases. A goal has to be envisioned, but this is only the beginning. The goal must be valuated and assessed in relation to other goals. It must arouse motives that generate the urge and intention to work toward it. Motives are seen as something active. They are aroused by the values that we attach to the goals we attain.[52]

Conclusions

Clearly, the debate over the existence and nature of the human will has been, and continues to be, a most complicated one. After reviewing the development of the debate from three different perspectives, there has been no real closure at all. We have found those who believe that whereas we have free will, it is only through divine grace. There are those who believe we have free will, but think it has nothing at all to do with God. God gets in the way of human will and robs humans of what should be theirs—power. There are those who do not believe there is free will at all; human beings behave according to their external surroundings. Finally, there are those who believe that not only does will exist, but it can be strengthened and conditioned to serve us better. And no doubt there are other possible perspectives as well.

What has this to do with the Black woman? Black women in slavery were robbed of human dignity. They were treated as chattel, as work horses, as animals. Her body did not belong to her, and the children she bore out of rape and forced "breeding" were more often than not taken from her. All that the Black slave woman had was her will.

From an African American perspective, many of the questions that Western theologians, philosophers, and psychologists have asked and addressed do not seem even remotely relevant, and they are not. Those Western perspectives are, however, the foundation for all contemporary American study. Western scholars continue to base discussions of self-will on these foundations and, unfortunately, African American theologians and scholars have been forced to consider this framework as the basis for any serious dialogue on the nature of self-will. Recently, Black theologians have resisted Western conceptualizations and have called for a "Black theology." It is in this spirit that this study moves toward a Black conceptualization on the nature of self-will.

A Black minister commenting on the question of creation vs. evolution pointed out that in an African frame of thought the existence of God is a given. He said that from the African world view everything comes from something.

> If an African were walking down a path and on the path he spotted a fine watch, he would pick up the watch, examine the fine craftsmanship, and although he had never seen anything like it before he would think, "somewhere there is a fine watchmaker!" The same is true for God or a Supreme One. When a person examines themselves and the perfection of their being, one must think, "somewhere there is a great people-maker!"[53]

Therefore, questions about the existence of God and the relationship of Black people to God is understood differently in the African American world view.

There is also the understanding that connections and interrelatedness are the life of the community. The sharing of experiences has been essential to the survival of the Black community. The understanding that one is not alone in pain and tragedy is important.

> The willingness to laugh in the face of misfortune without denying the seriousness of adverse reality is part of the survival equipment of Afro-Americans. Soul is the ability to laugh while growing with hardships, paying dues, and transcending tragedies.[54]

If this is true, Black women have been the soul of the Black community. They were forced to become disciplined, to set aside their desires for the future of their children, their families, and their community. Often that called for the single-mindness of purpose, endurance, and patience. Great courage was required because the stakes for the goals set were often high. Katie Cannon uses the terms invisible dignity, quiet grace, and unshouted courage[55] to identify the qualities of Black women which make them a model of the human will.

Chapter 2

The Phenomenological Method and the Concept of Will

What Is Phenomenology?

The study of a human phenomenon such as the will requires a research methodology that enables the researcher to explore the phenomena as these manifest themselves in human consciousness. Phenomenology has generally been defined as the study of the constitutions of human consciousness.

> Phenomenology is, in the 20th century, mainly the name for a philosophical movement whose primary objective is the direct investigation and description of phenomena as consciously experienced, without theories about their causal explanation and as free as possible from unexplained preconceptions and presuppositions.[56]

Martin Heidegger writes that phenomenology is derived from Greek, a combination of phenomenon and logos, which roughly translates to "let that which shows itself be seen from itself in the very way in which it shows itself from itself." Simply stated, phenomenology means "to the things themselves!"[57]

This definition helps us understand why, in particular cases, phenomenology should be used as a research methodology. Human beings are not completely formed and static, but are always in the process of becoming. In phenomenology, "the exploration and investigation of a phenomenon is an ongoing, open-ended process of coming to feel, experience and 'conscious' better what we have preciously felt, experienced, and 'consciosued' in part."[58]

The use of phenomenological research methods is not new; it is an important development in the history of philosophy in that for many students and readers of philosophy it is the "clearest exposition of what they had been thinking or trying to think all along."[59] "Phenomenology . . . poses the question of how the phenomenon arises in the presently structured world of human consciousness within ordinary experience."[60]

Phenomenology, rather than searching for empirical generalizations, seeks to grasp the intuitive essences of the phenomenon as they present themselves to us.

> Phenomenology neither designates the object of its research, nor characterizes the subject matter thus comprised. The word merely informs us of the "how" with which what is to be treated in this science is handled. To have a science "of" phenomena means to grasp its objects in such a way that everything about them which is up for discussion must be treated by exhibiting it directly and demonstrating it directly.[61]

We create meaning in our world not by the things alone, but by our experiences with the things, the object world. Through our experiences, we form concepts and these concepts are not the things at all, but "they are the meanings or structures forged by the mind in its experience of the things."[62]

By reflecting on our experiences one can flesh out the processes of awareness that normally remain hidden and "see again" the phenomena as it emerges. Each person

> lives within the meaning-endowing acts themselves and are aware only of the objectivity constituted in them, i.e., objective meaning. It is only after . . . [I turn] away from the world of objects and direct my gaze at my inner stream of consciousness, it is only after I "bracket" the natural world and attend only to my conscious experiences within the phenomenological reduction, it is only after I have done these things that I become aware of this process of constitution.[63]

Phenomenology takes no phenomenon as a given, but suspends all presuppositions; that is, holds every presupposition under scrutiny and examination. The researcher must even suspend all assumptions regarding the phenomenon until it has been carefully reflected upon and described. Therefore we can understand Husserl when he stated that we "tend to look upon the world as completed, constituted, and to be taken for granted. When I do this, I leave out of my awareness the intentional operations of my consciousness within which their meanings have already been constituted."[64]

Thus phenomenology assumes that the world in all its objectivity has meaning as humans within their own experiences give meaning to it. For the study of a concept such as will that means so much, that constitutes itself, and that grows in people so many different ways, I believe that no other method can even begin to reveal the essence of what the will really may be.

The Seven Steps of Phenomenological Reserach

Herbert Spiegelberg outlined seven steps or phases to the phenomenological approach. They are as follows:

1. Investigating particular phenomena. This step has three operations: (a) intuiting the phenomena – this involves carefully focused attention on the phenomenon while remaining sensitive to variations in the phenomenon which may have been hidden before; (b) analyzing the phenomena – this examines the phenomenon in relation to other phenomena (a kind of a sorting process) which determines if what we have thus far intuited is actually an example of the phenomenon; if so, how is it so? and (c) describing the phenomena. Examples of the phenomena are carefully produced.

2. Investigating general essences. From the descriptions of the phenomena in step one, particulars are drawn out to be further reflected upon. One might ask, What are the similarities in the examples of the phenomena that have been produced and reflected upon? Which examples and descriptions can be grouped together?

3. Apprehending essential relationships. This step is used to determine what is absolutely essential to the phenomena. This step requires use of the free imaginative variations to separate what is absolutely essential from that which is relatively essential or somewhat related, but not essential to the phenomena.

4. Watching for modes of appearing. Here what appears in consciousness and how it actually appears is explored. An object or concept does not always appear as a whole. Sometimes as perspectives change different aspects of the phenomena become visible. Sometimes the phenomenon never fully presents itself, but may remain obscured as if in a fog or haze.

5. Exploring the constitution of phenomena in consciousness. This step is used to disclose the typical structure of the phenomenon by examining the steps by which it is formed in consciousness. What pattern does it take on as it develops in the person's consciousness?

6. Suspending belief in existence. Here is where all presuppositions and beliefs of the observer are "bracketed off." This allows for further intuiting analysis and description of the phenomena.

7. Interpreting the phenomena. This final step involves the hermeneutic interpretation of the meaning of the phenomena. The goal is to discover meaning that may not be directly discernible.[65]

These seven steps are guidelines. They are not fixed, and many researchers choose to eliminate some of the steps. It is important to note, however, that Spiegelberg claims that all phenomenologists have made use of the first four steps, although not all have used the remaining steps. It is important for the researcher to remember that constant reflection is crucial. In each instance, the researcher intuits the phenomena; analyzes the phenomena; describes the phenomena; brackets off assumptions; then returns to intuit, analyze, and describe some more. "It is reflexive in that thinking constantly turns back upon itself. It is a self-critical process."[66]

Hermeneutical Interpretation

The final "step" described by Spiegelberg is the hermeneutic process or the interpretation of the phenomenon. Many researchers choose not to follow through with interpretation. However, this study makes broad use of the hermeneutic process.

Hermeneutics is generally defined as the study of the locus and principles of interpretation. The process was used particularly with ancient texts. Theologians and Biblical scholars refined the process and used hermeneutics primarily as a guide to be followed in exegesis of biblical texts. For these scholars, "the hermeneutical problem was focused on the study of each biblical document, both the literary context and the wider situation in which it appeared."[67]

Later, hermeneutics took on a broader meaning. Modern hermeneutics was greatly influenced by theorists such as Wilhelm Dilthey, Friedrich Schleiermacher, and later, Rudolf Bultmann, who became a modern leader in the field. According to Bultmann, hermeneutics refers to "the attempt to span the gap between past and present – a gap not only temporal but also cultural, dealing with world views and ways of thinking."[68]

When scholars worked with a text, the aim was to understand the text as itself. The scholar, therefore, was to be open-minded, removing himself or herself from the process in order give as unbiased a reading as possible. By using traditional hermeneutics, the scholar attempts to understand the text as the author wrote it, keeping in mind the cultural and historical context in which the text was written.

Hans-Georg Gadamer further refined hermeneutics. In *Truth and Method*, Gadamer suggests that it is not enough to merely understand a text. What we must really strive for is the "truth" or the meaning of the text. To do this, we must approach the text with all of our biases, presuppositions, and prejudices in place, for these are the things which make meaning possible in the first place.[69] Gadamer speaks of "horizons of meaning" and believes that it is only by "fusing horizons" that true understanding can take place – that is, fusing the horizon of the past (the author's horizon of meaning) with the horizons of the interpreter.[70]

Hermeneutical Interpretation as an African American Tradition

Hermeneutical interpretation is very much a part of the African American oral tradition.[71] African American preachers, teachers, and storytellers have often relied on their gifts of interpretation to make the Word live in their congregations, classrooms, and meetings. Black people who have been raised to appreciate the "gift" of the person who can "talk that talk," judge the speaker as much on his or her ability to interpret a complicated idea or text as the content of the text itself.

Hermeneutics as a Black Preaching Style

It is not enough for the Black preacher to read text and to prepare a good, well-organized sermon. The Black preacher also has to be able to "break it down," which means interpret the text in a way that relates directly to the congregation. According to the Reverend Dr. Henry Mitchell, hermeneutics, to Black preachers, is a code word for putting the gospel on a "tell it like it is, nitty-gritty basis." A good sermon will "hit home."[72]

Mitchell contends that ordinary Black men and women remain religious to this day because "they have been able to do so in their own relevant Black ways – in the context of their own religious experience."[73] The church was the one place where Black people could gather together and be themselves without drawing too much attention from the "white folks."

Data Collection

The data for this study were derived from two sources. The first source involved the interview material. (See the Introduction for a full explanation.) The second data source is the literature of four contemporary African American female novelists. The novel has often been a major vehicle for self-expression in the Black experience. Through writing, African Americans have confronted stereotypes and described their own experience, even if the events had to be fictionalized to make them less painful.

Important themes emerged as the writers developed the female characters in their novels and short stories, for these authors often created heroines who were composites of all the significant women in their lives and the experiences that most deeply moved them. The selected authors were Maya Angelou, Zora Neale Hurston, Toni Morrison, and Alice Walker. These four women were selected because they each have a unique writing style and they cover a broad spectrum of themes, relationships, and points of view.

Phenomenology enables the researcher to describe the phenomenon as it appears. The initial themes may or may not prove to be essential structures. The essential structures are those themes which are most vital or basic elements of the phenomenon.

From the novels, themes of will were extrapolated and then compared with the themes revealed in the personal interviews. Whereas eight themes were found to be of significance in the writings, only four of the themes matched those found in the interviews. Follow-up interviews suggest that while some of the women may have had experiences similar to those of the fictional characters, they did not place as much importance on these events. Some of the women felt that the authors may have dramatized certain things for the sake of the reader. While all eight of the themes are shared in this study, only the four themes or essential structures were further analyzed using the phenomenological approach.

After the essential structures are identified, they can then again serve as themes; but now the themes are considered structures essential to the phenomena rather than descriptors of them.

Phenomenology and Concepts of Will

We can begin to take a closer look at the concept of will by using the first step of the phenomenological approach, investigating particular phenomena. The phenomenon is will and from the preceding chapter many aspects or characteristics of will have already been identified. They can now be reexamined. A more careful focus may prove that these aspects are essential essences of the will.

The words "free" and "freedom" were often mentioned in relation to will. Free will, the freedom of choice, and freedom to act were all general themes throughout the debate. How free are we at all? Freedom may only be an illusion. Where does freedom come from? God? Or do we make our own freedom? With freedom, there is also responsibility. Perhaps responsibility is another important aspect of will.

Other words used frequently in the discussion of will were "self-determination" and "self-causation." What does this mean? Does it mean that we exist only because we will it? What does it mean to exist, to be? Is physical presence enough to justify being or does one exist only through actions and interactions with the object world? If a person ceases to act, does that person cease to be? Are people really what they think they are? These questions are important to consider.

"Power" is also used in describing will, especially creative power. Power, force, and energy all seem to be related to the human will. Does will give power or does power increase the will? According to Nietzsche, both would seem to be true.

From an African American perspective, one must add connectedness to the list of descriptive words, connectedness with one another in the context of a people of struggle and connectedness with the Supreme Being.

Black theologian and mystic Howard Thurman writes, "The human spirit seems inherently allergic to isolation. It can not abide a sense of being permanently alone or stranded in all the vastness of the universe or lost in the midst of the complexities of personal experience."[74]

We share our lives, and struggles with family, friends, and community and from this sharing gain the strength to struggle some more. We dream and by sharing those dreams we "keep the dream alive."

"Struggle" is another important theme in an African American context. As the Black community struggles with societal structures which crush the spirit and ultimately separate families and community, "struggle emerges as a way of life."[75]

Conclusions

The phenomenological approach is an appropriate method for the study of a concept such as the human will. This approach will allow the will to be studied as it emerges in the consciousness of individual human beings. By intuiting, analyzing, and describing the will as it appears, a deeper understanding of the African American woman is possible. We may not determine exactly and completely what the will is. This exactitude and completeness has not been done, although it has been debated for centuries. We will, however, understand much more clearly what it means to speak of one's will.

Some words of description have already emerged as starting points for the investigation. Words such as "freedom," "choice," "self-determination," and "power" have been frequently used to describe the nature of the will. Other words, such as "connectedness," "sharing," and "struggle," have been added.

The following chapters will introduce more themes and expand on the process of understanding the relationship between the will-to-succeed and the successful African American woman.

Chapter 3

Will as Seen in the Literature of Black Women

Themes of Will in the Heroines of Black Literature

When black women told the stories 'bout their real lives and actual experiences, they proved the power of art to demolish stereotypes; and if power is the ability to name one's own experience ... a first step toward power, for it celebrated the legends of black women, weaved dreams into myths that allowed us to recover and name our own past.
— Mary Helen Washington[76]

It is important to understand the often subtle courage and power of the African American woman. This is best revealed in the literary works of contemporary African American female writers.

Black female writers, as participant observers, capsulize on a myriad of levels, the insularity of their home communities. Due to systemic, institutionalized manifestations of racism in America, the Black community tends to be situated as marginated islands within the larger society. The perpetual powers of white supremacy continue to drop down on the inhabitants of the Black community like a bell-jar – surrounding the whole, yet separating the Black communities' customs, mores, opinions and system of values from those in other communities. Black female authors emphasize life within the community, not the conflict with outside forces.[77]

Black female writers, such as Zora Neale Hurston, Alice Walker, Toni Morrison, and Maya Angelou have created powerful images of African American women with all of their strengths, weaknesses, tragedy, and beauty revealed. Black female writers have combined in their characters all the qualities that have helped Black women, men, and children "get over" since slavery and by doing so have challenged the stereotypical images African American women have borne.

In this chapter, the writings of Black female writers will be reviewed in a search for themes of will that can be intuited, analyzed, and described. First, the fictional writings of Zora Neale Hurston, Alice Walker, and Toni Morrison will be reviewed. Each of these women has made major contributions to Black literature.

In Part 2 of this chapter, I will review biographical literature. I have chosen to concentrate on two very noteworthy women. Zora Neale Hurston will once again be the object of scrutiny. This time, however, Hurston's own story will be the focus. Zora Neale Hurston was a major force in the Harlem Renaissance. As an anthropologist, novelist, and collector of Black folklore, she traveled throughout the South. She was flamboyant and somewhat eccentric according to some, but she was her own woman and she did things her way. She suffered greatly for it and died penniless, betrayed by her Black colleagues.

Zora Neale Hurston did not die before she left behind part of herself that would live in other writers who would follow her. Alice Walker was greatly influenced by the life and legacy of Hurston. She made a pilgrimage to Hurston's home and placed a marker on her grave. Many themes of will can be found in the life of Zora Neale Hurston.

Part 3 will examine the life of Maya Angelou as told in her series of autobiographical works. Angelou has had a life full of all the tragedies, struggles, failures, and sufferings with which any black woman born poor can identify. But she has overcome, and the story of her triumph is an inspiration.

PART 1. THEMES FOUND IN THE FICTION OF BLACK FEMALE WRITERS

The Writings of Zora Neale Hurston

The works of Zora Neale Hurston celebrate the folkways and mores of the African American people of the rural South. Zora Hurston spent a lifetime collecting the stories, legends, myths, and songs of her people to prove that a different culture does indeed exist among Black people and that this culture is as complex and sophisticated as Anglo or European culture. Zora did not feel that she was a deficient human being from an inferior race of people. She had little patience with the Black leaders of the time who focused on the problems of Black people rather than recognizing and reinforcing the richness of Black life. As Alice Walker writes, "The quality I feel is most characteristic of Zora's work: racial health – a sense of black people as complete, complex, *undiminished* human beings...."[78]

This feeling of racial pride and well-being came naturally for Zora Neale Hurston. She grew up in the all Black town of Eatonville, Florida. The city was not only populated by Blacks, it was also governed by Blacks. There were small businesses that the people of the town supported. Zora Neale's experience of the South was very different from that of many African Americans of her time. Throughout her life she held onto what some considered an idealized view of the South and she was sharply criticized for it.

Zora was conservative by today's standards. She was critical of the Civil Rights Movement, integration, and desegregation. Her views stemmed not from a belief that Blacks and whites should remain separate, but rather because she celebrated the rich tradition and culture of her own people and felt that it would be lost through integration.

Hurston's life is an example of strength of character and unlimited courage. She used her own life as a backdrop for her fictional works. Hurston and her fictional counterparts acknowledge the raw coarseness of life. They face life squarely, front and center, without reverence or protection by the dominant powers in society.[79] This characteristic has been given the name "quiet grace" by Katie Cannon.[80] Because of their unprotected state, Black women have never been able to give in to anger, rage, and fear. They often have far too much on the line.

> The Black woman's very life depends upon her being able to decipher the various sounds in the larger world, to hold in check the nightmare figures of terror, to fight for basic freedoms against the sadistic law enforcement agencies in her community, to resist the temptation to capitulate to the demands of the status quo, to find meaning in the most despotic circumstances and to create something where nothing was before.[81]

Each woman Zora Neale created tried to carve a little piece of the world out for herself in some way. They all had "quiet grace." What is most interesting, however, is how each woman grew in grace and courage. Zora Neale Hurston, drawing from her own experiences, brought to life these women and the circumstances that shaped their lives.

Women in Love

Missie May: A woman in love. "The Gilded Six Bits," a short story, was originally published in 1933, a year before Hurston published her first novel. The main character is Missie May, a newly married young woman. Missie May is different in many regards from the characters Hurston would later create, but only on the surface. Underneath Missie May's soft, domestic exterior lies a woman with practical wisdom, strength, and bold determination.

Missie May is the "perfect" wife. She scrubs the floors and the stoop every Saturday morning. She cleans her home; cooks the food; and then bathes in order to great her husband, smiling when he arrives home from work. When teased by her husband, Joe, she proudly says,"Ah'm a real wife, not no dress and breath. Ah might not look lak one, but if you burn me, you won't git a thing but wife ashes."[83]

At first glance, one might think this is the statement of a weak, submissive, or at best an unliberated woman, and one can condemn the whole story as being sexist. The point is, however, that Missie May really loves her husband and wants to make a nice home for them. She is not acting because she has to; she wants to do these things. This was not really unusual for a woman of those times. She really feels that she and Joe are pulling equal loads – he works hard at the fertilizer works; she works hard at home. Missie May is confident in what she does and comfortable with herself.

The same cannot be said of Joe. When the slick-talking city man, Otis Slemmons, arrived on the scene, all of Joe's insecurities surfaced. Otis appeared to be prosperous. He opened an ice cream parlor in town. He had a big belly (a sign of good eating); he spoke of the big city, Chicago, where he had lots of women. Most of all, he had gold money. It was this money that really hooked Joe; he liked him and envied him at the same time.

Missie May was not taken in by either Slemmon's appearance or his talk. She tried to warn Joe, "His mouf is cut cross-ways, ain't it? Well, he kin lie jes' lak anybody else."[84]

Out of love, Missie May did a foolish thing. In an attempt to restore Joe's "manhood," she devised a scheme to get the gold coins out of the hands of the "undeserving" Slemmons and into the hands of her more deserving husband. Slemmons, whose plan was to bed Missie May, promised her the gold coins. Neither one expected Joe to return early from the fertilizer plant. Joe threw Slemmons out, but not before Slemmons dropped the coins in a plea for his life.

The coins turned out to be nothing more than gilded six bits. Slemmons was a fake just as Missie May had said. What happens next is interesting and finally gives us a clue to Missie May's devotion. Joe is silent for a long time. He discovered Slemmon's fraud when he had a chance to take a good look at the coins. Yet he said nothing to Missie May.

Missie May cried at first; she realized she had greatly jeopardized a happy marriage. Then, after she realized that Joe was not going to throw her out, she settled into his silence. Only once did she think of leaving; but as she left the house, she ran into Joe's mother and went back home. "Never would she admit defeat to that woman who prayed for it nightly. If she had not the substance of marriage she had the outside show."[85]

No one, least of all Joe's mother, expected much from Missie May. She had a mother who used to "fan her foot round right smart"; it was expected Missie May would do the same. Part of Missie May's devotion was true love for Joe, but part of it was a desire to rise above everyone's expectation of her. Missie May decided to wait out the silence. She knew that if she stuck it out Joe would come around one day. He did. Joe also loved Missie May a great deal. He came to realize the truth of her words and trust more in himself and the relationship they had together.

Mother's Love

Zora Neale Hurston expanded upon the same "mother wit" and folk wisdom she learned in her childhood and characterized in Missie May and developed it into her first novel. *Jonah's Gourd Vine* was first published in 1934 and was a part of a period that brought Hurston much acclaim and also much criticism. While the novel has the Reverend John Pearson as its central character, it is still a statement about the power, wisdom, and courage of a Black woman.

Amy Crittenden: The power of mother's love. The novel begins with "John Buddy" Pearson as a big, strong 16-year-old. At this time, it is his mother, Amy Crittenden, who is the central figure in John's life as a protector and advisor. John would continue to be protected by women all of his life. Amy is married to Ned Crittenden, an older man and a harsh man, who abuses all of the children but John in particular because it is quite obvious that John is not Ned's child. Amy had John before marriage and judging by his fair skin, he is probably the son of Marse Alf Peterson, Amy's former master when she lived "over the big creek."

This knowledge eats away at Ned, but it also brings out the steel in Amy. She stands up to her husband when he threatens to beat John Buddy and lets him know how far a mother will go to protect her children:

> Ned Crittenden, you raise dat wood at mah boy, and you gointer make
> uh bad nigger outa me.... Ah don't mind when he needs chesstizin' and
> you give it tuh 'im, but anytime you tries tuh knock any dese chillun 'bout
> dey head wid sticks and rocks, Ah'll be right dere tuh back dey fallin'.
> Ah'm dey mama.[86]

Later, when Ned expresses the resentment he feels for the attention Amy gives to the children, she replies with this bit of practical
wisdom:

> . . .we ain't got tuh let de white folks love our chillen fuh us, is us? Dass
> jest de pint. We black folks don't love our chillun. We couldn't do it when
> we wuz in slavery. We borned 'em but dat didn't make 'em ourn. De
> b'longed tuh old Massa. 'Twan't no use in treasurin' other folkes prop-
> erty. It wuz liable tuh be took uhway any day. But we's free folks now.
> De big bell done rung! Us chillen is ourn. Ah doan know, mebbe hit'll
> take some us generations, but us got tuh 'gin tuh practise on treasurin'
> our younguns. Ah loves dese heah already uh whole heap. Ah don't want
> 'em knocked and 'buked.[87]

The theme of domestic violence is one that prevails in the writings
of African American authors. Amy's analysis of this sad tendency toward
violence by Black males is insightful for it links domestic violence to the
violence of slavery. Amy did not really fault her husband; he was coping
the only way he knew how. Both Amy and Ned had been slaves and, therefore, had probably either experienced or seen the lash used as an instru-
ment of control. For many men like Ned, power and the lash were almost
synonymous.

Amy understood that years of negative behaviors would have to be
unlearned. In the meantime, she made her stand; she was willing to jump
in between anyone and anything that would harm her children, beginning with her husband. For Amy, the love she had for her children and
the ability to finally keep her children as her own, care for them, and protect them gave her power.

The relationship that exists between Black mothers and their children
is an important theme. If any judgments can be made from Amy's statement, it would be that once Black mothers dreaded motherhood; but
after slavery, they realized their children and families would no longer
be torn apart. As mothers, they had the power to protect those they loved;
they cherished the role. The strength that Black women seem to draw
from their children is often tremendous. Statements like "I look at my
children and I have to keep going" and "If I can't do it for myself, I'll do

it for the child" are testimonies to the strength of the relationship between mother and child.

This theme of mother's love will recur. In the case of Amy Crittenden, this love was not enough to protect John Buddy. Ned, unable to control his resentment of the "yaller" boy, arranged to lend John Buddy over to a white planter who was known for his cruelty. Amy was not able, in this case, to keep her child; but she helped him get away and told him to go "over de Big Creek" where everyone knew her. It was "over the creek" that John met his father, Marse Alf Pearson, who gave him a job. John, in turn, took on his last name and was John Pearson thereafter. It was also "over the creek" that John met the other woman who would place an important role in his life, Lucy Potts.

Lucy Potts Pearson: The power of truth. John crossed over the creek at age 16 with just the clothes he had on his back. The first person he met was Lucy Potts as she played with her classmates in the school yard. Lucy was a bright-eyed girl, pretty and smart, with a quick humor that endeared her to all; John immediately fell in love. She was the joy of her parents for it was well known that she was the smartest girl in the school.

Over the next years, John Pearson worked, played, went to school, and waited for Lucy to grow up. Lucy and John had a mild courtship during these years despite the fact that Lucy's family did not approve. They had much more in mind for their child than a "stray nigger" from over the creek. Lucy defied her parents, for she had also fallen in love with the big, strappin' John, the only person who had every outrun her and was strong enough to protect her. John as a man was a charmer. He had a way with words which he learned to put to use with women. He finally proposed to Lucy with these words, "Lucy, don't you worry 'bout yo' folks, hear? Ah'm gointer be uh father and uh mother tuh you. You jes' look tuh me, girl chile. Jes' you put yo' 'pendence in me. Ah means tuh prop you up on eve'y leanin' side."[88]

Lucy succumbed to the sweet words and married John Pearson. But John could not be faithful to Lucy however much he loved her. Before their first child was born, John was well in a pattern of chasing women and spending money. Lucy was aware of John's straying and told him, "if you loves her de bes', John, you gimme our chillun and you go on where yo' love lie."[89]

In the years that followed, Lucy stayed with John and was there to back him up on "eve'y leaning side." Three days after she delivered her fourth child, she got her husband out of jail. ". . . Mist' Perkins Ah come tuh see 'bout mah husband. . . . Ah come wid jus' whut Ah stand in, 'cause Ah ain't got nothin' else, but Ah come."[90]

After this incident, Alf Pearson encouraged John to pack up his family and move on, hoping a change of location would remedy John's woes. So the Pearsons moved on and settled in West Florida. There John put his gift of poetic speech (heretofore used for wooing women) to praising the Lord. Yet the Reverend John Pearson had as many problems as before. As a preacher, he was even more popular with the womenfolk. Soon he was back to his old ways and when the church elders were talking, once again Lucy was there. Lucy's shrewd judgment and faith that truth never fails is evident in the following passage:

> You preach us sermon on yo'self, and you call tuh they remembrance some uh de good things you done, so they kin put it long side de other and when you lookin' at two things at de same time neither one of 'em don't look so big, but don't tell uh lie, John. If youse guilty you don't need tuh git up dere and put yo' own name on de sign post uh scorn, but don't say you didn't do it neither. Whut you say, let it be de truth. Dat what comes from de heart will sho reach de heart agin.[91]

This passage, more than any other, gives a clue to what drives Lucy Pearson and that is her perception of "the truth." To some, Lucy might seem weak and long suffering, putting up with a no-good husband; but if one analyzes Lucy's "truth," one finds this is not the case at all. Lucy knows John is unfaithful, but she can "call tuh her remembrance" some of the good things he had done. These good things were the truth to her; the other was John's attempt to live a lie. She believed in the truth that her husband loved her; and she knew that emotionally, of the two, she was the stronger.

Lucy's sorrows finally sapped her strength and her health failed her; but as she lay dying, she confronted her husband. The power of her words so affected John that he did something he had never done in all his years of marriage, he struck her. He could not bear to come into her room after that, her will was too strong and he felt condemnation in her very presence. So he sent the youngest daughter, Isis, in to bring out reports on her dying mother.

Lucy knew her time was short, but she was not afraid.

> . . . Ah done put on the full armor uh faith. Ah ain't afraid tuh die. Don't worry about me. . . . Ah done been in sorrow's kitchen and Ah done licked out all de pots. Ah done died in grief and been buried in de bitter waters, and Ah done rose agin from de dead lak Lazarus. Nothin' kin touch mah soul no mo'.[92]

The characters of John Pearson and Lucy Potts so closely resemble what little is known about Hurston's own parents that it can be said that in writing *Jonah's Gourd Vine* Hurston was trying to come to grips with some of her unhappy past. She was the young Isis of the story. The one who tended her dying mother and the one that received the parting wisdom of Lucy Potts Pearson (Hurston). Lucy Hurston told the young Zora the very words that she was to later write:

> . . . member tuh git all de education you kin. Dat's de onliest way you kin keep out from under people's feet. You always strain tuh be de bell cow, never be de tail uh nothin'. Do de best you kin, honey. . . . Don't love nobody better'n you do yo'self. Do, you'll be dying befo' you' time is out.[93]

These words were to later take Zora Neale Hurston a long way. She heeded her mother's words. She was able to fight against the odds for her mother had prepared her for battle. But she was comfortable and confident with herself and always strained to be the "bell cow."

The Power of Vision

Their Eyes Were Watching God, published in 1937, is considered Zora Neale Hurston's finest work. This novel, like many of Hurston's works, draws from the Black folk tradition of the rural South. Much of the novel takes place in Eatonville, Florida, the home of Zora Neale Hurston. And while the names of the characters are different, they closely resemble the actual men and women of Eatonville whom Zora loved so much.

The novel is the love story of Janie Crawford, who eventually finds love and fulfillment when she meets and later marries a younger man, Vergible Tea Cake Woods. Even this scenario of a woman in love with a younger man is drawn from Hurston's own past, for she had a rather stormy affair with a younger man just prior to writing the novel. Again Zora used her writing for therapeutic purposes. Although Tea Cake is a very different man from Hurston's lover, she admits trying to capture the essence of their relationship – the tenderness and passion.[94]

Janie Crawford: Patience and the power of a dream. Zora Neale Hurston begins the novel by describing the difference in the way a man dreams and the way a woman dreams:

> Ships at a distance have every man's wish on board. For some they come in with the tide. For others they sail forever on the horizon, never

out of sight, never landing until the Watcher turns his eyes away in resignation, his dreams mocked to death by Time. That is the life of men.

Now, women forget all those things they don't want to remember, and remember everything they don't want to forget. The dream is the truth. Then they act and do things accordingly.[95]

At the beginning of the story, Janie Mae Crawford returns to Eaton-ville, Florida, from the Everglades. All of the townspeople are standing around waiting, ready to judge her. They think she is returning because she has been defeated, and they are ready to condemn her. But Janie has not been defeated; she has triumphed because for a short while she had lived her dream.

Janie was the product of a dream, her grandmother's dream. Nanny wanted everything for Janie that she herself had been denied as a slave. She wanted for Janie an easier life, a life free from abuse and the toil and struggle of a slave woman. To Nanny, only a good marriage to a man with property and money would insure that Janie would not be treated like "de mule of de world." She arranged for 16-year-old Janie to marry Logan Killicks.

At 16, this was not Janie's dream. As she was beginning to blossom as a woman, Janie dreamed of a blossoming pear tree much like the one that grew in her backyard. Lying up under the tree, she could feel the breeze. She discovered the secrets of pollination and longed for this kind of union that would make her feel the fullness and delight of a blossoming being. She wanted a marriage, but not a marriage to an old man. Not for land or money did she want to marry a man she knew could not fulfill her.

Janie married Logan Killicks, thinking that after the marriage she would love her husband. She would be like the bee and the pear tree; she wouldn't be lonely any more. Her grandmother died a happy woman, believing that "her" Janie was a protected woman. Nanny could rest in peace knowing that Janie would not have to be a "work ox" or a "brood sow" and that Janie could "look upon herself and never have her feathers crumpled by folks throwin' up things in her face."[96]

Janie, once married, waited for the love to come. Killicks tried very hard at first to please her, but there was nothing to really draw them together. In less than a year, Janie discovered that "marriage did not make love. Janie's first dream was dead, so she became a woman."[97]

Janie continued to dream and to search for her own truth and in that search she found Joe "Jody" Starks. Joe was a person with big dreams.

He came to Janie telling her about an all–Black town in Florida called Eatonville. He was going there, and he wanted Janie to come too.

Janie left Logan Killicks and followed Joe Starks in search of his dream to the town of Eatonville, Florida. Eatonville was just a small hamlet when Joe Starks arrived with his wife, Janie. But he soon changed all that. He bought land and then sold it as lots, recruiting families to come and share in the dream of an all–Black city. Joe opened a store, which was not only the business center of the community, but the social center as well. "Jody" Starks was a big man, and when it came time to elect a mayor, Joe was the people's uncontested choice.

Janie followed Joe expecting adventure, and she found herself just "marking time." She discovered that Joe wanted her as a pretty possession. He wanted her on a pedestal, the envy of all of the townspeople, out of the reach of all save himself. He, Joe Starks, had to think for her, tell her what to do for she could not be trusted to think on her own. Women did not think, "they just think they's thinkin'."

In time, Janie stopped expecting anything out of her relationship with Joe ("Jody"). She lived a comfortable life as far as material comforts were concerned; Jody saw to that. But the dream didn't really go away. It was during this time that Janie discovered she could live outside herself.

> Then one day she sat and watched the shadow of herself going about tending store and prostrating itself before Jody, while all the time she herself sat under a shady tree with the wind blowing through her hair and her clothes. Somebody near about making summertime out of lonesomeness.[98]

Janie, when faced with a loveless marriage, a life that seemed doomed to be unfulfilling and unchallenging, did what many Black women have done under the circumstances. She in many ways split her life in two. On the surface, she was "Miz Janie Starks," wife of the mayor, someone to be looked up to. On another level, she was plain Janie Crawford, a woman with dreams no one could understand, a woman with feelings no one could touch. Janie on the outside lived within the restraints of being the mayor's wife. On the inside, she was a woman in waiting, living for the day when her two lives could come together into one. She reinvented and redefined herself in order to keep her sanity.

Janie's opportunity came soon enough. Joe Starks died. He rotted away without ever understanding the real Janie, the Janie beyond his assumptions of what a woman should be. He never understood her resentment of him and the cage he had built around her. He expected her to be grateful. When she was not, he turned hateful. His last moment was one of agony, trying to fight death long enough to make Janie pay.

Janie's life came together when she met "Tea Cake" Woods. He allowed Janie to be herself. He set no limits on her and often challenged her to try new things, especially if it was something they could do together. Tea Cake and Janie left Eatonville and headed to the Everglades for the challenge offered by the cane fields. There they worked side by side, not because Tea Cake wanted Janie to labor like a "mule of de world" but because they couldn't stand to be apart from each other too long. Janie's dream of the perfect union, the bee in the pear tree, was a reality at last.

The dream was not to last too long, however. While trying to flee a terrible hurricane, "Tea Cake" was bitten by a rabid dog. When the illness finally consumed him, Janie had to shoot her own husband to save herself.

After a short trial where she was found not guilty, Janie buried "Tea Cake" in a grand style and returned to Eatonville. The people thought she came back defeated, but as Janie told her friend, Phoeby, she was back victorious. She still had the money that Joe Starks had left her, and she had lived her dream. She had memories enough to last a lifetime.

The Works of Zora Neale Hurston in Retrospect

Zora Neale Hurston not only celebrated the great folk traditions of African American people in her writings, but also contributed several important themes for understanding the Black female and her capacity for survival. The first theme is that of love. The love embodied in characters like Missie May is not a weak, insipid sort of love, but rather a determined love. It is a love built on emotion, but guided by common sense.

The second theme is the power of mother love. Amy Crittenden understood the pain of having no power to protect the children one brings into the world. The ability to have children is a creative act, and the ability to hold on to and protect that creation is a natural right. Amy understood that power is passed on generation to generation, mother to child.

The third theme is the power of truth. Lucy had little else to sustain her than the power of the truth as she knew it. Lucy had a moral code which she developed from her own knowledge and understanding of the world. She had the truth of her experiences. She also understood that it did no good to lie to people, to pretend to be something that you could not be. The truth would out and the lie would destroy. The truth might be painful, but it would allow healing to take place. In the end, this was all she could pass on to her young daughter.

The last theme is that of holding on to a dream and having the patience to wait on the dream to come true. Janie Crawford knew that a perfect union was possible, she'd seen the mating of the bee in the pear blossom. When her first marriages failed to offer complete fulfillment, she did not throw away the dream. Janie lived outside her dream, surviving on a day-to-day basis; but the dream was always there in the back of her mind, making it possible for her to keep on struggling.

While each of these heroines must deal with very complicated circumstances, Zora Neale Hurston's folk style makes the characters themselves very easy to understand. These are everyday women who do what they need to do without fanfare. They are heroines without being heroic.

The Writings of Toni Morrison

As we turn to the writings of Toni Morrison, we can see how, through her use of symbolism and some rather complicated metaphors, characters emerge that affect the reader in a powerful way. Toni Morrison's women haunt with their intensity, her stories captivate with their chilling reality.

Toni Morrison's characters portray women who have the capability to make tough, courageous decisions. Her novels are rich in metaphor and allusion and often have to be read on two levels. Even the names of the characters often have symbolic meanings, like the Peace women from the novel *Sula*, who were anything but peaceful; Pilate Dead from *Song of Solomon*, who was as unusual as her name would suggest; and the ghost child in *Beloved*, who was a daughter that no mother could love.

Morrison's heroines are sometimes enveloped in themes and motifs which may seem gruesome and destructive, but the actions they take must be weighed against the outcomes these women achieve. Hidden under rough exteriors are women who are no less vulnerable. The novels of Toni Morrison depict the black persona encased in a world which heaps upon them a conglomeration of ideals, images, and experiences which the reality of their lives belies. Characters are forced into creative responses to their nonconventional experiences.[99]

The term "psychological disorientation"[100] has been used to describe characteristics found in Morrison's women because of the way in which they deal with the inconsistencies of life. The characters tend to laugh at what is not funny and (at least on the surface) do not seem to understand the ironies in their lives. If one could make a generalization about Black females based on the portrayals in Ms. Morrison's novels, it would be that they had to become somewhat schizophrenic to survive.[101]

Morrison feels that the behavior of her characters is not schizophrenic or irrational at all. It is perhaps extreme or excessive, but there is a logic to what her characters do, and by their actions they depict an important part of Black style.[102]

Black humor often has little to do with what is funny and what is not. It is a coping mechanism. It is not merely laughing away one's troubles either. It is much deeper than that. Morrison calls it being able to see the underside of something and credits the ability to do this as a strength that has helped Black people stay alive and fairly coherent despite duress.[103] It is the ability to take the worst situation and find something valuable in it or to turn it into your own joke that you know the "boss man" doesn't understand.

The women in Toni Morrison's novels are indeed powerful. They have the ability to heal and the ability to destroy. Not one character is passive; each one plays an important role in developing themes of will, survival, and triumph. An examination of three central characters from the highly acclaimed novel *Sula* will reveal two more important themes of will.

Friendship and Survival

The lives of the two main characters in the novel *Sula* are so interrelated that it is somewhat difficult to separate them. The novel is about the friendship between Nel Wright and Sula Peace. They were an unlikely pair. Nel was very quite; Sula was loud and daring. Nel grew up in a rather staid traditional household, while Sula grew up in what Nel thought was a much more exciting home. The Peace women loved a good time. These two very different girls became friends and the novel traces the bonding of these women. The theme of connectedness is revealed throughout the novel. Toni Morrison very skillfully illustrates the beauty of a friendship between the girls and just as skillfully shows us the destruction that can take place when friendship is lost, when the connection is broken.

Nel Wright and Sula Peace: "We was girls together." "We was girls together... O Lord Sula."[104] These are the words of agony and understanding that the woman Nel uttered the day her friend Sula died.

Sula and Nel grew up together in Medallion, Ohio, a town which was as unlikely as their friendship. Here every year on the third of January, the town celebrated National Suicide Day led by Shadrack, a man who was left a little crazy after World War I.

The Black section of town was called the Bottoms, even though it actually set high in the hills above the town of Medallion. But that was a joke. Once again, the white "Massa" had won when he tricked his slaves into settling in hilly land, leaving him the rich, fertile valley floor.

The people of Medallion were pleased with the result; the valley might have been the better farmland, but the Bottoms were more beautiful. For the residents of the Bottom, maybe the last laugh was on "Massa."[105]

It was in this defiant atmosphere that Nel and Sula came together. Nel lived in a neat ordered home. Her mother, Helene, worked hard to erase the memories of her childhood as the daughter of a New Orleans prostitute. Since she could not control her own past, she felt compelled to control and manipulate her husband and daughter. At her mother's funeral, Helene finally felt free. Nel accompanied her mother to the funeral and at that point established her autonomy. She was herself – she did not want to merely be her mother's daughter, but she wanted to be recognized in her own right.

It was not long after this that she met Sula and they became friends. In the beginning, Helene did not approve of Sula because she did not approve of Sula's mother, Hannah; but as time went on, Sula was always welcome. Sula had a way about her that was bright and easy. Her easy nature came from growing up in a household where

> a pot of something was always cooking on the stove; where the mother, Hannah, never scolded or gave directions; where all sorts of people dropped in; where newspapers were stacked in the hallway, and dirty dishes left for hours at a time in the sink, and where a one-legged grandmother named Eva handed you goobers from deep inside her pockets or read you a dream.[106]

The girls got along famously. As typical friends, they played together, went for ice cream together, and grew interested in boys together. The girls "felt the ease and comfort of old friends. Because each had discovered years before that they were neither white nor male and that all freedom and triumph was forbidden to them, they had set about creating something else to be."[107]

The girls were also typical in that they shared secrets, except their secret involved murder. Sula and Nel were playing down by the river with a young boy they called "Chicken." Sula was teasing the boy and picked him up, twirling him around and around. Suddenly she let go, hurling the boy into the water. Chicken disappeared. His body was discovered later that afternoon.

Nel witnessed all of this; the only other person who may have seen was Shadrack, who everyone knew was insane. Nel did not tell on her friend. Neither girl ever mentioned the incident, but the knowledge tightened their bond.

This incident was the first indication that something was a little bit strange about Sula. She never showed any remorse for Chicken's death; curiosity, but not remorse. In fact, except for the genuine regard Sula seemed to have for Nel, she seemed never to feel anything at all.

Sula was emotionally disconnected. Even though she lived in a house which was lively and full of people, she lacked the one thing that may have tied her in to all the people surrounding her, her mother's love. This was not really Hannah's fault. Hannah was a free spirit, lazy, easy-going; she loved everybody, men in particular. She gave herself away in a way that endeared her to all the men. She had such a cheerfulness and innocence about her that the men's wives accepted her. She had, therefore, little left over for Sula.

Sula found out how her mother felt by accident when Hannah was discussing children with another woman, "I love Sula. I just don't like her." These words sent Sula "flying up the stairs."[108] When she came down she had no feeling in her heart. It didn't show at first on the outside, but later even Nel would become aware that Sula was missing something. Later, Sula watched Hannah burn to death with the same sense of curiosity that she had when she drowned a small child.

The friendship continued on into adulthood. Nel married and Sula went away. It was upon her return that things changed between the two women. The tie was severed.

Sula's return was an unusual event. Her returning was marked by a "plague of robins." The coming of the birds can perhaps be taken as an omen of the destruction which will follow.

Nel was happy to see Sula though. They took up like they had never been separated. Nel was married and had children, but her friend's return was "like getting the use of an eye back, having a cataract removed." Nel felt her better self coming out in the presence of Sula and some of her girlhood humor returning. Nel attributed their friendships to the fact that "Sula never competed; she simply helped others define themselves. Other people seemed to turn their volume up when Sula was in the room. More than anything humor returned."[109]

But the laughter would not last long. Knowing that Nel loved and trusted her husband, Jude, Sula seduced him. Knowing this was the one thing that would really hurt Nel, Sula was quite callous. She didn't even really want him and rejected him after he and Nel separated. Nel could not forgive Sula. Sula would never really connect with anyone again.

Nel was not totally unscathed by the separation. She developed a "puff" or sort of pressure in the back of her eye which did not go away until the day of Sula's funeral.

Sula died in a strange way – her body rotted, as if the disease in her mind suddenly took over her body as well. Before she died, Sula gave full vent to her emotions. She

> lived out her days exploring her own thoughts and emotions and giving them full reign, feeling no obligation to please anybody unless their pleasure pleased her . . . experience taught her there was no other that you could count on . . . there was no self to count on either. She had no center, no speck around which to grow.[110]

Sula had Nel for a center once and felt let down by her when she discovered that she and Nel were not the same person. She reached out only once more, this time to a man named Ajax. She and Nel had known him since they were girls. Ajax used Sula and then left her. After that, everything was gone and Sula rotted away.

Before Sula died, Nel visited her. They talked about the friendship they had. Nel wanted a confession or an apology so that she could grant absolution. She didn't get it. Sula was not sorry. All Nel got was Sula's scorn when Nel questioned her about her relationship with Jude: "And you didn't love me enough to leave him alone. . . . You had to take him away." Sula responded, "If we were such good friends, how come you couldn't get over it?"[111]

When Sula died, however, she was calling the name of her only friend.

Reflections on friendship. The theme of friendship and the importance of intimacy are very dramatically delivered in *Sula*. In a very powerful way, Morrison is saying that we must be connected. We all strive for intimacy; it is a lifelong search, true. As Sula discovered, there is no one that is the same as self; but we must know ourselves at the same time we seek to know others. Through life, as we grow we should as well grow closer to understanding ourselves and at the same time increase our capabilities of understanding others.

Sula had some very important ties severed early. She never understood herself, for as Toni Morrison said, she had no center. Sula gave reign to the fury inside her, and it ate her away. The destruction of a friendship in Sula's case was also the destruction of her will.

Eva Peace: Sacrifice and survival. Eva Peace was a survivor. She was the heart and soul of the Peace household. Sula inherited from Eva boldness and a free spirit, but none of her genuine love and selflessness. Eva's behavior in many ways was as excessive and strange as her granddaughter's; but while Sula's intent was to destroy, Eva's actions were for the survival and well-being of the family unit.

Eva Peace was a young woman when she married "Boy Boy" and had three children, Hannah (Sula's mother), Pearl, and Ralph, who she called Plum. At that time, Eva had two legs and the story of how Eva happened to lose one of her legs was a remarkable tale that gained Eva much respect in the Bottom.

After five years of marriage, Boy Boy left her and her three children. She had no money and, although the few neighbors understood her situation and tried to help, Eva and her children were hungry. After the baby, Plum, got sick and Eva had to literally use her hands to open up his bowels, Eva decided what she must do. She left her three children with a neighbor, saying she would be back the next day.

> Eighteen months later she swept down from a wagon with two crutches, a new black pocketbook, and one leg. First she reclaimed her children, next she gave the surprised Mrs. Suggs a ten-dollar bill, later she started building a house on Carpenter's Road, sixty feet from Boy Boy's one-room cabin, which she rented out.[112]

The fact that one of Eva's legs was missing was rarely mentioned; people tended to just ignore it, the one she had left was beautiful and shapely. The rumor was, though, that Eva had laid her leg across a train track and later collected $10,000 insurance money. This was enough to get Eva over the hard time and insure comfort for herself and her children in the years to come.

Boy Boy returned a few years later for a visit. Eva discovered at that time that she hated him, perhaps for the desperate action to which his leaving drove her. But in that hate she found another reason for living.

> Knowing that she would hate him long and well filled her with pleasant anticipation, like when you know you are going to fall in love with someone and you wait for the happy signs. Hating Boy Boy, she could get on with it, and have the safety, the thrill, the consistency of that

hatred as long as she wanted or needed it to define and strengthen her or protect her from routine vulnerabilities.[113]

While her hate for Boy Boy hardened her and guaranteed her survival, it also sent her upstairs to her room. After Boy Boy's visit, Eva slowly retreated up the stairs to rule her household from the confines of her bedroom. She sat in a small wagon which made her surprisingly mobile. From the wagon, she entertained her various friends, for Eva was very popular, especially with the men. She played checkers and rented rooms to anyone coming through who needed a place to stay. The house was always filled with people so Eva found very little reason to come down from her room, except on two occasions – once to light a fire and the other to try and put one out.

Eva's youngest child, Plum, was her favorite. She had hoped to leave everything to him; but Plum went off to war and when he returned he was addicted to drugs (probably heroin). Eva waited awhile and slowly saw the signs that her child was drifting away, the drug altering all signs of the child for whom she had sacrificed so much. One night, Eva went down the stairs slowly and painfully on her crutches. She held her son close in her arms, crying for what had been. Then she dowsed him with kerosene and set him on fire. Hannah found the burning Plum and cried to Eva that Plum was burning, but they couldn't open the door. Eva's only response was, "Is? My baby? Burning?" The life she had saved out of love she ended when she realized that in many ways he had already died.

Ironically, Eva's oldest child also burned to death, but this time Eva risked all in trying to save her. Later, Eva said that she saw the signs; something terrible was going to happen. Hannah was doing the fall canning and the dress she wore got too close and burst into flames. Eva saw her catch fire from her upstairs window:

> . . . there was time for nothing in this world other than the time it took to get there and cover her daughter's body with her own. She lifted her heavy frame up on her good leg, and with fists and arms smashed the windowpane. Using her stump as a support on the window sill, her good leg as a lever, she threw herself out of the window. Cut and bleeding she clawed the air trying to aim her body toward the flaming, dancing figure. She missed and came crashing down some twelve feet from Hannah's smoke. Stunned but still conscious, Eva dragged herself toward her firstborn . . . [114]

Hannah died a tragic, painful death while her mother crushed her body in trying to save her, and Hannah's daughter watched unmoved.

Eva survived this tragedy. But in the end, her granddaughter proved to be her undoing. When Sula returned to the Bottom, she had Eva put away in a nursing home knowing she was helpless to stop her. Yet in the end it was Sula who rotted away. Eva survived her children and her granddaughter, a testimony to her endurance.

Final Reflections on Toni Morrison

While on one level one could argue that Toni Morrison's characters are unnatural or uncommon, on a deeper level they symbolize human needs and emotions that are very natural. Human beings search a lifetime for intimacy and friendship. Many, like Sula, believe they will find a person who is as close to them as they are to themselves. When Sula found that this could never be, she began to destroy herself. Sula had nothing to hold on to, for she never knew herself and she didn't understand that the first love must come from within. The message of Toni Morrison is clear: "Women must seek to become their own historical subject in pursuit of its proper object, its proper and specific expression in time."[115] Unless a woman can understand and define herself, she is apt to destroy herself.

Eva Peace understood herself very well, and she exemplifies the need every human being has to survive. She had to sacrifice something in order to survive, but the loss of a limb was better than the slow death of starvation. She also felt a responsibility for her children whom she loved. In her mind, warm hugs and kisses were not the indicators of love that others feel are so important, it was what you would do to insure that they lived, survived in a world that had little regard for those without means. Even her murder of Plum was an act of love in her mind. She had already given him all she had. She could do nothing to help her baby son this time. In her mind, the quick sure death of the fire was better than the equally sure but slow death from drugs.

Friendship and survival are two themes which Toni Morrison presents in a very powerful way as themes of will in both a positive and destructive manner. As we move on to the writings of Alice Walker, we will see how these same themes can be expressed in a different way.

The Writings of Alice Walker

Alice Walker is perhaps one of the most well-known Black female writers of our time. Part of her appeal is that she writes from her own understanding and identity as a Black woman. She has experienced oppression herself and believes that all Black women are among the most oppressed people in the world. Alice Walker tells us why she believes this every time she puts her pen to paper. Mary Helen Washington refers to Alice Walker as a great poet, novelist, short story writer, critic, essayist and apologist for Black women.[116]

> What particularly distinguishes Alice Walker in her role as apologist and chronicler for Black women is her evolutionary treatment of Black women; that is she sees the experiences of Black women as a series of movements from women totally victimized by society and by the men in their lives to the growing developing women whose consciousness allows them to have control over their lives.[117]

Sisterhood

Nowhere is this evolutionary pattern more evident than in the novel *The Color Purple*,[118] where once again we encounter the theme of friendship. As the story unfolds we understand the complexity of human relationships. The lives of Celie, Mr. _____, Shug, Sofia, Harpo, and all the others are revealed as a rich tapestry – each person a separate thread but intertwined. The bonds of kinship and friendship draw these people together; and in the end, each one is strengthened and encouraged by being connected with the others.

In the beginning, Walker tells the story of the woman, Celie, who is the "mule of the earth." She suffers the physical and mental cruelty that has been the burden of Black women. Celie is both narrator and victim. We can feel through her the pain of a woman who is powerless to fight against the oppression of racisim and sexism.

It is natural that Celie tells her story in letters written to God. Like many other Black women, it is through a constant conversation with God that day-to-day existence is maintained. Celie was a "suspended" Black woman.[119] She survived from day-to-day by living like one who is sleepwalking. In this manner, she could survive being raped by her father; having the children she bore snatched from her arms almost at birth; being married off to a man whom she neither knew nor loved; taking care of the children of a man who did not love her or appreciate her attention; and having the one person who did love her, her sister, sent away. Celie had to suspend all of her feelings just as many other Black women did who were

> suspended in time and place by a century, an era that only acknowledged them as laborers, these women were simply defeated in one way

or another by the external circumstances of their lives. For such women – the great-grandmothers of the black women of contemporary times – pain, violence, poverty, and oppression were the essential content of their lives.[120]

Celie's life changed after Shug Avery came to live with Celie and Mr. _____. Celie was always attracted to Shug even before she met her. She knew that Shug was her husband's lover, but that was no problem for Celie did not love her husband. She was fascinated, however, by the fact that there was a woman who could make her cruel husband jump; a woman who would dare to wear fancy clothes, smoke, drink, and sing those sultry songs that were unfit for churchgoing people to hear.

When Shug came to live with them, she taught Celie how to love. She helped Celie become comfortable with herself and to love herself. She helped her see the good which was inside her and to acknowledge all the hurt and anger she had kept bottled up inside her for so many years.

Shug and Celie shared their pains and triumphs. Celie began to understand that she and Shug were alike. They were "sisters" in suffering; they merely suffered in different ways. Celie had lost her family; Shug had lost hers too. But while Celie remained fairly innocent, Shug had lost her innocence long before. Shug was wise in the ways of men and women; she knew how to use their strengths and weaknesses.

When Shug found out that Albert beat Celie, she made him stop. When she found out that he had been hiding Celie's letters from her sister, Nettie, she found them and in many ways gave Celie back her sister. When Celie was angry and could no longer write to God because she had lost her faith, Shug shared her God with Celie and allowed Celie to believe again. Celie replaced her old image of a God who was white, male and sat on high and judged Black women, with a God that lives within the heart of each person. Finally when the time was right, Shug took Celie away from the farm and to the city to find a life of her own.

At the end of the story, it is a different Celie who is reunited with Nettie and the children who were taken from her. The new Celie is a confident woman. She understands herself and therefore can better understand others. She has even reconciled her bitterness and anger at her husband. She knows now that his cruelty toward her was out of his own weakness and ignorance. She also knows that she doesn't have to take his abuse just because she is a woman. By understanding Albert better, she can let go of hate.

The lives of Sofia and Squeak are also interwoven in this story. Each of these women do their part to help Celie on her climb from a victim to a victor. Though it would ordinarily seem very unlikely for Sofia and Squeak to be united in any way (Sofia is the wife of Albert's son, Harpo, and Squeak is Harpo's lover after Sofia leaves him), the point is that the understanding and compassion Black women have for each other is often very deep.

Sofia was a young girl, only 15 years old, when she married Harpo. She was a strong, hearty girl, pretty and solid. She loved Harpo dearly and had five children by him. But life had taught Sofia that in order to survive one had to fight. She was determined not to let anyone beat her. She would defend herself and her dignity. She shared her feelings with Celie, but at the time Celie was so beaten down she could not understand. Celie was somewhat jealous of Sofia at first. Sofia did what she wanted to do and she would fight. Celie didn't believe she could fight; she admitted to Sofia that she had never before struck another human being.

Harpo wanted to make Sofia mind. Even though he and Sofia were happy and loved each other, Harpo felt that he was the man and Sofia should do what he said. He asked his father and Celie what he should do. Celie, out of jealousy, told Harpo to beat her. Later Celie could not sleep at night for the wrong she had done.

> What is it? I ast myself. A little voice say, Something you done wrong. Somebody spirit you sin against. Maybe. Way late one night it come to me. Sofia. I sin against Sofia spirit. I pray she don't find out, but she do.[121]

When Sofia finds out and confronts Celie, they find that as Black women, as sisters, they can relate to each other despite their differences in approach. For each woman is trying to do the same thing – to survive in a world that would beat and destroy them. Celie confesses her weaknesses and, in doing so, they find laughter which binds them together and makes living possible.

Sofia: What you do when you git mad?

Celie: I think. I can't even remember the last time I felt mad, I say. I used to git mad at my mammy cause she put a lot of work on me. Then I see how sick she is. Couldn't stay mad at her. Couldn't be mad at my daddy cause he my daddy. Bible say, Honor father and mother no matter what. Then after while every time I got mad, or start to feel mad, I got sick. Felt like throwing up. Terrible feeling. Then I start to feel nothing at all.

Sofia: Nothing at all?

Celie: . . . Well, sometime Mr. _____ git on me pretty hard. I have to talk to Old Maker. But he my husband. I shrug my shoulders. This life soon be over, I say. Heaven last all ways.

Sofia: You ought to bash Mr. _____ head open. Think about heaven later.[122]

The laughter which followed this exchange allowed Celie to sleep comfortably again. They had healed each other's hurts by acknowledging each other's plights and then finding a reason for laughter in the midst of their pain.

Sofia eventually left Harpo. He continued in his attempts to bend her to his will, and she grew tired of fighting him. Although she left Harpo, she did not leave the family fold. This reveals another unique characteristic of many Black families. The extended and inclusive Black family is often made up of ex-wives and sometimes their new spouses. Sofia was still connected and loved because of the 12 years she was married to Harpo and the five children she bore him. Harpo himself still loved Sofia even though life went on and he took in a new woman, Squeak.

"Squeak," as she was called, received her nickname from Harpo. It described her high-pitched voice and her generally mousy manner. Harpo could tell Squeak what to do. Sofia's life was to be joined with this woman's life in a way that neither of them ever expected.

Sofia met with a downfall. One day when she was out with her children, the mayor's wife insulted Sofia by asking her if she wanted to be her maid. When Sofia responded with a hearty "Hell, no" the mayor struck her for sassing his wife. Sofia, true to her nature, could not take a lick and let it go. She hit back. Before it was over, Sofia was in jail after being nearly beaten to death.

The whole family was concerned; Harpo was miserable. Sofia was fading fast in the jail where she was being bitten by rats and worked to exhaustion in the laundry. It was decided that Squeak would go and talk to the white warden, who it turned out was her uncle. The plan was to get Sofia out of jail by saying that Sofia deserved worse punishment. What would hurt Sofia more would be to make her serve out her time as maid to the mayor's wife. Squeak went and gained Sofia's release to the custody of the mayor's wife, and she was raped by her "uncle" in the process.

When she returned to the family and told how she had been raped, she spoke up for herself for the first time. If she could be raped to save her lover's wife, then she deserved to be called by her given name, Mary Agnes.

Sofia was away for 11 years. During that time, Mary Agnes helped raise her children, along with Harpo and Sofia's sister. When Sofia was finally released, the children did not really remember her. They called Sofia's sister "Mama" and called Squeak "Little Mama."

But Sofia got another chance to raise a child. Squeak (Mary Agnes) by this time had been encouraged by Shug to start a singing career of her own; she had a good voice. So she decided to leave Harpo and go with Shug to Memphis, but she had to make provisions for the daughter she would have to leave behind. Sofia quickly told Squeak to go on and sing. She would help Harpo raise Squeak's little one.

The compassion and understanding which flows from woman to woman is an important theme which no writer deals with better than Alice Walker. The feelings of kinship and friendship that are so hard sometimes for outsiders to understand are essential. These relationships have been sources of strength that Black women have frequently used to renew their will.

Alice Walker: A Look Back

Alice Walker writes of the Black woman as an individual in the making. Because of the violence of sexism and racism, the Black woman had to hide the energy and beauty that lay within her soul. This creative energy always seemed to emerge in some way though, too powerful to be totally masked. Some women planted flowers; some kept a spotlessly clean house, hiding peeling paint and paper with a picture or a vase; some women sewed and quilted as Celie did. But the energy was there.

Women of the next generation are a little freer. In Walker's first book, *The Third Life of Grange Copeland*,[123] she portrays Ruth as a woman of this next generation. She saw her mother, Mem, murdered at her father's hand. Mem tried, but she had all her dreams dashed away by illness and oppression. Ruth would not have to deal with the violence. Ruth is from the next generation of Black woman who would have more opportunities.[124]

Alice Walker, when asked about the evolution of her characters, says:

> My women, in the future, will not burn themselves up–that's what I mean by coming to the end of a cycle, and understanding something to the end ... now I am ready to look at women who have made the room larger for others to move in.... I think one reason I never stay away from the Southern Movement is because I realize how deeply political

changes affect the choices and life-styles of people. The Movement of the Sixties, Black Power, the Muslims, the Panthers . . . have changed the options of Black people generally and of Black women in particular. So that my women characters won't all end the way they have been, because Black women now offer varied, live models of how it is possible to live. We have made a new place to move. . .[125]

PART 2. THEMES OF WILL FROM BIOGRAPHICAL WRITINGS

Zora Neale Hurston: How It Feels to Be Colored Me[126]

Zora Neale Hurston was one of the driving forces of the Harlem Renaissance. She celebrated in the culture and traditions of her native South and never lost sight of her roots there. She was the life of any party; entertaining her friends for hours with the stories about the people in her home of Eatonville, Florida. Joe Clark, Lige Moseley, Daisy Taylor, and Aunt Caroline (Cal'line) were probably as familiar to some of her friends as they were to Zora herself. Yet for all her flamboyance, Zora remained an enigma to many people. She was a stark individualist who, while appearing open and exuberant on the outside, guarded much within.

Proof of her guardedness is that no one, not even those who were closest to her, knew her exact age. Zora changed her birth dates constantly. Depending upon whether she was trying to impress someone with her youth or her age, she claimed to be born in 1898, 1899, 1900, 1901, 1902, or 1903. Because birth records of the period did not survive, no one is really sure, though it is generally thought that she was probably born in 1903.[127] Even in her own autobiography, *Dust Tracks on the Road*, there are many unexplainable discrepancies; and it is clear that Hurston wanted to remain somewhat a mystery.[128]

What is known is enough to determine without a doubt that Zora Neale Hurston was a strong-willed and determined woman. She lived her life with no real apologies and few compromises. She was a complex woman who in some way managed to balance the contradictions in her life. This didn't always make her the most popular person in her circle; she was in fact often the subject of harsh criticisms. A friend once remarked, "Zora would have been Zora even if she was an Eskimo."[129]

Zora's confidence and well-being came primarily from growing up in Eatonville, Florida. This town was a self-sufficient, all–Black town. Zora's own father, John Hurston, had once served as mayor. The community nurtured young Zora. She never grew up with a feeling of inferiority as many young Black children do. She knew without a doubt that Blacks could hold responsible positions; they worked hard for a living and lived full, rich lives.

For Zora, white people were a novelty – people to be wondered about but not feared. She did not experience the harsher effects of racial prejudice and discrimination or feel the bitter oppression that leaves one feeling powerless and inferior. Zora's experience of the South was novel, and her experiences gave her great self-confidence and confidence in Black people. Some of her later very conservative positions also grew from these same experiences and brought her much criticism. But whatever Zora Neale Hurston's experiences were, they prepared her to do battle with the world, to make a place for herself, and to challenge the assumptions that had previously been held about her people. It is clear that Zora Neale Hurston was a woman with a destiny.

Zora Neale Hurston: A Woman of Destiny

According to Hurston's own autobiography, *Dust Tracks on a Road*, she knew at a very young age that she had a special purpose. Zora's destiny was revealed to her in visions that she said began when she was about 10 or 11 years of age. These visions or premonitions served to prepare her for later events:

> Like clearcut stereopticon slides, I saw twelve scenes flash before me, each one held until I had seen it well in every detail, and then be replaced by another. There was no continuity as in an average dream. Just disconnected scene after scene with black spaces in between. I knew that they were all true, a preview of things to come, and my soul writhed in agony and shrunk away. But I know that there was no shrinking . . . I knew my fate. I knew I would be an orphan and homeless. I knew that while I was still helpless, that the comforting circle of my family would be broken, and that I would have to wander cold and friendless until I had served my time. I would stand beside a dark pool of water and see a huge fish move slowly at a time when I would be somehow in the depth of despair. I would hurry to catch a train, with doubts and fears driving me and seek solace in a place and fail to find it when I arrived, then cross many tracks to board the train again. I knew that a house, a shotgun-built house that needed a new coat of paint, held torture for me, but I must go. I saw deep love betrayed, but I must feel and know it. There was no turning back. And last of all, I would come to a big house. Two women waited there for me. I could not see their faces, but I knew one

to be young and one to be old. One of them was arranging flowers such as I had never seen. When I had come to these women, then I would be at the end of my pilgrimage, but not the end of my life. Then I would know peace and love and what goes with those things, and not before.[130]

This passage is an example of the clarity of description which was characteristic of Zora Neale Hurston. She was convinced that there were certain events in her life over which she had no control. Perhaps this also served to make her in many ways fearless. She later wrote that she saw each one of the visions played out. Unfortunately, this is unclear from reading *Dust Tracks*. She begins relating the visions, but doesn't follow through with the theme. She only gets to vision seven or eight and leaves one to wonder about the rest.

At the death of her mother, her first vision was realized. Lucy Hurston was much the same as Lucy Pearson in *Jonah's Gourd Vine*. She is described as being a strong, wise woman who loved learning herself and encouraged her children to get a good education. She favored Zora and on her deathbed told her to "jump at de sun." She also told her she knew things were not going to be easy for her; she would have to suffer much but that she would be all right. In this way, Zora was well prepared for the struggle that lay ahead.

After her mother's death, she was virtually an orphan, for her father soon afterwards remarried. Zora and her stepmother could not get along and Zora left home. She lived between older siblings or worked as live-in help for the next few years, but it was a sad existence which later she remembers:

> I was doing none of the things I wanted to do. I had to do numerous uninteresting things I did not want to do, and it was tearing me to pieces. I wanted family love and peace and a resting place. I wanted books and school. When I saw more fortunate people of my own age on their way to and from school, I would cry inside and be depressed for days, until I learned how to mash down on my feelings and numb them for a spell. I felt crowded in on, and hope was beginning to waver.[131]

Zora rekindled her hope and in 1925 finally arrived in New York City where she immediately fell into Black literary circles. Zora had the opportunity before she came to New York to complete her high school education at Morgan Academy in Baltimore. She continued her studies at Howard University in Washington, D.C. While in Washington, she met and impressed novelist Fannie Hurst, who later asked Zora to be her secretary. Through her connection with Fannie Hurst, Zora met another novelist, Annie Nathan Meyer. Meyer was impressed with Zora's abilities as well and offered her a scholarship to Barnard College, a school she had helped found in New York.

This was a serious turning point for the young woman from Eatonville, Florida. While at Barnard not only did she make a place for herself among such Black talents as Alain Locke, Langston Hughes, and Richard Wright, who would be the "heart and soul" of the Harlem Renaissance, she also discovered anthropology, which would from then on be a passion of hers. Zora studied under the famous anthropologist Dr. Franz Boas while at Barnard.

Zora saw how the folk stories, songs, and rituals of her youth could be studied, collected, and brought to life for all to appreciate. Boas, who was confident of Zora's ability, sponsored her in her first data-collecting trip back to her homeland, Florida, after she completed her studies.

Zora also had another sponsor, Mrs. Osgood Mason. Mason, a wealthy widow, was patron to many of the Renaissance talents, including Langston Hughes. It is unfortunate that so many of the artists of those times had to rely on white patronage. While Zora received a good deal of financial support from Mason, it also meant that for many years she did not own her own work and she was a virtual slave to the woman. Some of Zora's greatest critics attacked her for her conduct during this period. They felt she acted like a "Tom" in many ways, whining and groveling at Mason's feet, begging for favor. This may be true or perhaps Zora was shrewdly playing a game of survival. But the fact is that few Black artists could be self-sufficient, so hers was the lot of many.

These were Zora's golden years. During this time, she went on several collecting ventures that took her not only to Florida, but to New Orleans and Haiti as well. There she collected data on voodoo or "hoodoo" practices, studying under the best voodoo priests and priestesses.

Zora found it difficult to balance her love of anthropology with her love of writing. She wanted to do something with all of the good material she was collecting. She was determined to make it somehow. Her tenacity is evident in the fact that she once wrote her patron, Mason: "I shall wrassle me up a future or die trying."[132]

And she did succeed. During the next 20 years, Zora would write and publish six books. Her life, though successful, would not be any easier. She often came under sharp criticism. She and once-close friend Langston Hughes would have a bitter disagreement which was never resolved. Once her ties with Mason were broken, she never again had real financial freedom.

Yet this did not daunt Zora. She was content to live a simple life and did not need much money. She did almost break, however, when in 1948 she was accused of molesting a young boy. Zora was hurt and left New York almost defeated, with nothing to fall back on, she wrote her friend, Carl Van Vechten, "I care nothing for anything anymore. My country has failed me utterly. My race has seen fit to destroy me without reason and with the vilest tools conceived of by man so far."[133]

The molestation charge was proved to be false and, in fact, Zora did recover. Once again, she had "been in sorrow's kitchen," but she did not remain there.

Zora Neale Hurston died January 28, 1960. She was penniless, but from all accounts not unhappy. She was still trying to write and had lived independently until illness forced her into a county welfare home.

A collection was taken so she could be buried in an unmarked grave. In 1973, Alice Walker had a tombstone placed on her grave reading:

Zora Neale Hurston
"A Genius of the South"
1901–1960
Novelist, Folklorist
Anthropologist[134]

Zora was a woman with a destiny and a will to match.

PART 3. THE AUTOBIOGRAPHICAL WRITING OF MAYA ANGELOU

The autobiographies of Black women are rich and valid sources for further studies of the Black woman and for critical inquiries into how she has viewed herself historically despite labels, myths, and ideas about her place and role. If any form of literature is capable of aiding in the Black woman's attempts to correct the record, it is autobiography, for nowhere does one find literature as a celebration of life more than here.[135]

Learning to Learn from Experience

If the autobiography has served as a celebration of life for the Black woman, then none have celebrated longer or with greater fervor than

Maya Angelou. In her four autobiographical works we witnessed the growth of a somewhat solemn, lonely child into an extraordinary woman. Maya Angelou spreads out her life before us and allows us to share with her as she remakes her life, her loss of innocence replaced with dignity, her never practiced delicacy, with quiet grace, and her forced responsibility, with unshouted courage.[136]

> Wouldn't they be surprised when one day I woke out of my black ugly dream, and my real hair, which was long and blond, would take the place of the kinky mass that Momma wouldn't let me straighten? My light-blue eyes were going to hypnotize them, after all the things they said about "my daddy must of been a Chinaman" . . . because my eyes were so small and squinty. Then they would understand why I had never picked up a Southern accent, or spoke the common slang, and why I had to be forced to eat pigs' tails and snouts. Because I was really white and because a cruel fairy stepmother, who was understandably jealous of my beauty, had turned me into a too-big Negro girl, with nappy black hair, broad feet and a space between her teeth that would hold a number two pencil.[137]

The feelings Maya Angelou expresses in this short passage are not unusual for a young girl who grew up in Stamps, Arkansas. In *I Know Why the Caged Bird Sings*, Maya Angelou (born Marguerite Johnson) spans the first 13 years of her life. She and her brother, Bailey, traveled to Stamps when she was three to be raised by her grandmother. Her parents had divorced. She remembers her father putting them on a train with tags bearing instructions attached to their wrists and tickets pinned inside her brother's coat.

Stamps, Arkansas, was far different from the Eatonville, Florida, of Zora Neale Hurston's youth. Stamps was racially segregated, with the Black families living across the pond and down the railroad track from the white families. Maya, as a young child, dreaded whites, realizing that the possibility of humiliation and cruelty was always present. She learned to stay within her place, relating to those in her own community as people and whites as "the other."

Her childhood was not entirely unhappy. Her grandmother owned a small store; its smells and sounds filled her childhood. She also had her brother, Bailey, whom she adored. He was everything that she thought she was not: small, graceful, and beautiful.

She also had her grandmother, "Momma," and her Uncle Willie. From her grandmother, she received the strict upbringing of a churchgoing woman. Momma valued cleanliness, respect, and dignity. She passed on these values to her grandchildren. She was a severe woman, but her love of her grandchildren was ever present. She was like many Black mothers who believed that there was a promised land beyond this life and that one had to discover within oneself the wit and resourcefulness to find strength in weakness, joy in sorrow, and hope in despair. She also believed that the love of a mother cannot always be determined by physical presence or material gifts. Frequently, that love had to be realized out of hardship and shared suffering.[138]

Young Maya learned these lessons from her grandmother and, therefore, always had something to fall back on. Her life story is one of constant defeat followed by victory, constantly building upon itself until by the end of her series, the reader forgets the defeats, but celebrates with great enthusiasm the victories.

Maya was also greatly influenced by her mother, especially as she grew older and left her home in Stamps. Vivian Baxter, according to Maya's accounts, was a beautiful, vivacious woman. She had the practical street wisdom of a woman who has "made it" on her own. She and her large family encouraged Maya in her pursuits: "Be the best of anything you get into. If you want to be a whore, it's your life. Be a damn good one. Don't chippy at anything. Anything worth having is worth working for."[139]

They had no sympathy for her, however, when she was down on her luck. As a result, Maya never really stayed down long. She cried and indulged in self-pity for a while, but knew that after a time she had to pick herself up and keep pushing on. This was what was expected of her. She later wrote: "They were a close-knit group of fighters who had no patience with weakness and only contempt for losers. . . . I congratulated myself on having absolutely the meanest, coldest, craziest family in the world."[140]

From this crazy family, Maya learned to be independent, resourceful, and to trust in her own ingenuity. This led her from a job as a fry cook to whorehouse madam to dancer to actress to writer. She never really reconciled herself to her too-tall appearance, but later saw her true beauty reflected in the eyes of her own child. She searched for love outside herself and triumphed when she found it within.

Maya Angelou continued to chronicle her life in three more works. Through her autobiographical writings, she reveals her continuing struggle to find a comfortable place for herself. Her willingness to write about her experiences—her rise from humble beginnings, her struggle with self-hatred, and her success and failures—have made her one of the most popular African American writers today. Her candor and grace have served as an inspiration to other Black women.

Conclusions

The themes of will which resonate from the writings of Black female writers are a link to understanding the Black woman. The themes I have elaborated on – romantic love, motherhood, practical wisdom, friendship, faith, dreams, patience, and vision – are not all the themes, but they appear to be the most essential ones to understand. How the Black woman sees these themes acted out before her as she grows from child to woman has a great influence on the person she becomes.

The themes which describe the heroines in the literature may or may not serve as essential structures for further phenomenological analysis. They are important descriptors, however, and provide a clear picture of the kind of strength and courage for which Black women are known. In the next chapter, themes from the lives of contemporary African American women will be described. By comparing the themes that emerge as these women tell their life stories to the themes from the literature, the essential structures of self-will are revealed.

Chapter 4

Themes of Will in African American Women

> Negro women, historically, have carried the dual burden of Jim Crow and Jane Crow. . . . These women have often carried disproportionate burdens in the Negro family as they strove to keep its integrity intact against the constant onslaught of indignities to which it was subjected. Not only have they stood shoulder to shoulder with Negro men in every phase of the battle, but they have also continued to stand when their men were destroyed by it. Who among us is not familiar with that heroic, if formidable, figure exhorting her children to overcome every disappointment, humiliation and obstacle. This woman's lullaby was very often "Be something!" "Be somebody!"
>
> — Pauli Murray

For many African American women, the quest for success has indeed been a fight. Black slave women, by nature of their birth, found themselves in a situation where they would always have to fight for whatever humanity they would attain. The understanding that struggle and resistance were a part of life was passed on from one generation to the next. And so the African American people survived. Paula Giddings writes that

> Black women had a double challenge under the new slavery: They had to resist the property relation which was different in form, if not in nature, to that of white women and they had to inculcate the same values into succeeding generations.[142]

The responsibility that Black women felt for passing on to the next generation a capability to withstand mental anguish, possible physical abuse, and assaults to their dignity took on characteristics that are not often understood by those outside the Black community.

This chapter will describe the four themes which are considered essential structures in the development of a strong self-determined Black female. These themes are "family relationships: the mother-daughter bond," Black women as sisters," "deep spiritual awareness," and "Black community connectedness." The words that are quoted come from real women. Each interview was confidential; therefore these women felt free to speak as they wished. The women spoke at length as they looked back and shared their life stories.

Black Family Relationships

In order to understand how the will emerges in African American women, one must go back to their roots. The family is the primary socialization unit for the Black child, much as it is in other cultures. However, unlike other cultures the family serves another purpose. Along with social mores and norms the Black child must learn how to survive within a society which has a long history of institutionalized racial hatred. For African Americans these lessons are crucial, for their ability to survive and cope relies upon how well they learn them.

Black family relationships have long been misunderstood; the structure of the Black family has even been regarded as pathological and unhealthy.[143] While the Black mother-daughter bond was particularly stressed in the interviews conducted, that in no way suggested that a matriarchal order exists or that men are any less valued. In many cases, the women felt that their male siblings were more valued and "pampered" by their mothers, while they themselves took on extra responsibilities.

Until certain economic changes take place and black males are able to compete on equal terms in the dominant culture without fear of reprisal, tensions will continue to exist that drive the Black male from the household. Clearly, the single parent family is one of the most crucial issues before the Black community.[144] "If a man isn't making any money, he doesn't want to be there at home, feeling useless." Until then, Black women without men will continue to use whatever resources they have to keep their families together.

African American Mothers and Daughters

"I am a strong, Black woman because I was raised by a strong, Black woman. It is a known fact that when a Black woman is determined, watch out. Nothing is going to keep her back." Statements like this one were repeated over and over again in the interviews conducted for this study. The fact that mothers are often very influential in the upbringing of their daughters is not significant in and of itself. Mothers in many cultures have the primary responsibility for child care and are thus very influential. What is different is the way in which many Black women were raised and the fact that the bond between mother and daughter often lasts long past childhood. Black women continue to draw strength from their relationships with their mothers and grandmothers and speak of the strong lessons they learned which "made" them the women they are. The dream and hope of a better tomorrow had to be passed on from one generation to the next. For the Black mother,

> ...children have represented the very special promise of freedom for an entire people. Even as Black people's efforts to hold on to and strengthen their family ties were cruelly assaulted, the family has remained an important cauldron of resistance, forging and preserving a vital legacy of collective struggle for freedom.[145]

"This meant in many cases a stern upbringing for their daughters, who had to be taught not to be seduced by favors, not to seek too much to please, not to let themselves be compromised."[146] Young African American girls had to be prepared in a special way if they were to have any chance at all to break free and create a space for themselves. According to Dr. Vivian Gordon, the majority of Black women have "managed to maintain a positive self-identity, and to experience some levels of success as mothers, wives, sisters, and daughters; as leaders, activists, women working outside of the home; and as women generally contributing to the quality of life within the African American community."[147]

A primary lesson that Black girls were taught was how to take responsibility for themselves and for the family. The notion of family unity and connectedness and interdependence is viewed as the unifying philosophic concept in the Afro-American experience.[148] Children who grow up in the Black family, which often includes parents, aunts, uncles, cousins, grandparents, and friends, are all linked together in a kinship network. The children grow up and are exposed to a cultural tradition where the emphasis is on survival. The family survives through collective responsibility, resourcefulness, and resilience.[149] The lessons and values of family life are passed from one generation to the next through a rich oral tradition. The Black mother has been the primary transmitter of the traditional culture and values of the Black family.

Within the context of the family, the Black female child is "constantly exposed to a cadre of women in authority and decision-making roles."[150] As these females grow up and see their mothers, grandmothers, aunts, and sisters take on heavy responsibility, they learn that they must be responsible as well. As one respondent said, "I think most black women, well myself, I think I get all of my strength and my hidden powers from my mother. I have seen my mother give birth to two of my sisters one day and the next day she was back on her job."

The Black female grows in confidence as she sees the good that comes from the mother's hard work:

> When I was young my mother and father started having some difficulties. My father decided that he was going to withdraw funds from the family. My mother went to work at a . . . I'll never forget, a raincoat factory, during the war. She was a piece worker. She'd come home at night, dead tired and together we'd figure out how much she had earned for the day. I started to look at her, how she reacted to things and how she carried herself. It was as if the whole time she was saying, "Hey, I'm keeping my family together, I will do what I have to do." So just to see what Momma was doing, working and standing on her own, not in some subservient role, it was very different. I started to tie into what my momma was doing because it seemed she had a good thing going.

The Black mother tries to instill this strong work ethic in her daughters because she knows that, for a little Black child, life is a struggle. In order to cope with hurt and defeat, the African American female must know that she will always have to work hard. For anything she gets she will have to work hard anyway. And sometimes, in spite of it all, she won't get the things she deserves. "All you get, you are going to have to go out there and earn, you are going to have to go there and take it. That's why I think very highly of myself, because everything I have I earned."

Tied in with the notion that hard work is the only way to transcend a negative environment is the belief that a solid education is also needed. Education is something to work hard for and many Black mothers sacrificed a great deal so that at least one child could go to school. Often after an older child was put through school, that child would get a job and was responsible for helping the younger siblings.

> Education was everything to my mother, you see she didn't have it. My mother probably went to eighth grade. I don't think Daddy even got that far. But all eight of my mother's children graduated from high school. Two of us went on to college. My sister finally finished college, she went back. I never did. I really didn't like school that much.
>
> I was an excellent student because my mother had been the teacher in this one-room school down South and so she taught us. She had us interested in reading. I remember one incident, I guess I was in first

grade. The teacher had us up to the blackboard to teach us how to write our ABCs. She put up a big "A" and said everybody make an "A." Well, my mother had already taught me my ABCs so I started writing. I was all the way to "F" before the teacher stopped me. She said, "You stand in the corner," and she put a dunce cap on my head. It was a long time, even after I became a teacher myself, before I understood why I was being punished. Of course, all of those teachers were white, no doubt they were racist, too, and they wanted to discourage the Black students. That sort of disillusioned me . . . fortunately for many kids that experience might have left a lasting imprint upon them, discouraging them, but apparently it didn't do that to me because I didn't let it phase me. I just kept on learning.

If the family was to advance, each generation had to go further in school than the one before. "It was very important, in fact that was the motivation of most Black families when I was coming along, that the children should advance further than them."

As a result of an emphasis on responsibility and achievement, many African American girls grow up with the confidence that when times get hard, they are not going to fall apart. They have no illusions that life is going to be easy; in fact, they know that the opposite is true. "You have to go out there and you have to work twice as hard as the white kids in order to even get a fair grade." But they can challenge the unfairness of a racist society because they have been prepared; and as long as the family unit remains intact, they can survive. "I remember my mother always telling me that no matter how much we fuss and fight and get on each other's nerves, I'm still your mother. You can always come back and see me."

Tough Love

To outsiders, it may seem that some of the lessons African American mothers pass on to their children are very harsh. But the intent is not cruel. Sometimes the Black mother feels compelled to be strict with her daughters out of love.

> I got pregnant with my daughter my senior year of high school, and I was unable to take the track scholarship I had received. So when I graduated, I immediately went into the work force. I had to get a job. I did graduate from high school; I had promised my mother that I would get my diploma. But I was really upset with my mother. I wanted to go to college. I felt I had an opportunity and she should take responsibility and raise my child. I was angry with everyone. Now I thank my mother because I feel if she had let me do what I wanted to do, I wouldn't be

the person I am today. Later, when my daughter was thirteen I did go
back to school and then Momma was a big help to me.

The lesson was hard; but by having her mother refuse to take care
of her child, this woman learned that she was truly responsible for any
mistakes that she made. Yet even though the mother did not make it easy
for her daughter, she still encouraged her and maintained high standards
for her. When this woman grew up and was serious about returning to
school, she found her mother to be her biggest support.

> I believe that you get out of your child what you put into your child.
> There's a lot of pressure out there being put on children and your child will
> be easily manipulated. But if she has that strong home sense of responsi-
> bility, and that strong pride, knowing that Momma is going to be there
> to catch her, or if I make a mistake Momma is going to be there for me, or
> if she really messes up Momma is going to be there to crack her on the
> head to make sure she gets straight! That is not going to stray too far.

As these Black females grow to adulthood, they remember the lessons
learned from their mothers and the other females who surrounded their
childhood. They continue to act responsibly because they don't want to "let
anybody down," but by now they have enough self-love that they do not
want to let themselves down. The cycle begins again as they prepare the
next generation. Black women take great pride in knowing that their
children have "done good" because they feel that they poured everything
they had into it.

> If you're a mother and you really love your children, then you know
> those children did not ask to come here and they don't know nothing. You
> owe them. If you really love your child then it's up to you to provide for
> that child and for that child's future and you have to be strong, you have
> to look out for the child.

Another woman said:

> I raised my four children, I did it. Their father helped because he worked
> and provided well for us and that enabled me to stay at home and raise
> my children. But I see myself in all that they do. It makes me feel good
> when my friends, and sometimes people I don't know tell me what won-
> derful children I have. I know I have good children, but it wasn't easy, it
> took a whole lot of cussing and a whole lot of praying.

The Role of the Father

While the father in most of the interviews played a lesser role in the growth and development of most of the women interviewed, there were some exceptions. For most of the women, the father had no real influence because he was not there. Single-parent households are not uncommon. Black male abandonment of the family has contributed to the struggle of the Black female who must go it alone without a mate.

The single parent household, however prevalent, is not the rule. Several women had two parent households; and while the father had a "different" place in their lives, these women found their relationships with their fathers to be important.

> My Dad always used to tell me, you can do whatever you want to do if you really want to do it. So if you are going to be a bum, be a good bum. He told me to if you want to have something, be independent. You don't have to wait around for somebody to do things for you, you can do it for yourself.
>
> When I was coming up my Daddy was there, when we got ready to do something we would go ask my father, but he would tell us, "go ask your mother," so we knew that my mother was really controlling the house ... but I talked to my father about everything. My mother had eight other kids that she had to deal with so I felt she didn't have time to fool with me. I took my problems to my Daddy. When he died, I was at a loss at first. Suddenly I found myself without that outlet, without someone to talk to.

In households where the fathers were present, they often shared the mother's concern that the female children were prepared to fight the racism and sexism they knew they would encounter. In the book *My Soul Looks Back*, the Reverend James Cone remembers his father teaching him and his brothers and sisters that "survival for black people requires constant struggle."[151] To prepare their daughters for the worst, racism was openly discussed in some households.

> The main barrier, of course, for me has been racism; but my parents started militating against that early. We always ate supper together and after supper we would sit around and talk about what had happened during the day. We would analyze it. Of course, that's not the language they used, but that's what we did. And my father would say something like two wrongs don't make a right and would we discuss how we could go back in there and do battle. So we were trained not to let those things that occurred get to us. We processed that in our family and figured out how we could get around and cope despite the social barriers that were

there. We learned to "make a way out of no way," how to work around the barriers.

Another woman speaks about how she grew closer to her family as a result of being confronted with racism in the schools.

>I remember when I was in high school. I went to an integrated high school. Most of the kids were the elite, upper crust nonminority students. I remember we all sat in alphabetical order. Except the blacks. We had to sit in the back of the room. And it was just – I don't know. I had never confronted anything like it before. My parents were working class. My mother made many of my clothes. The wealthy students dressed out of the finest stores. I remember one of the girls got a brand new Ford convertible on her fifteenth birthday. You know, that was very indicative of the kind of class I was in and I began to see a very clear separation.
>
>Getting back to the classes, we sat in the back of the room and when we raised our hand for a response, we were ignored just like we were vegetables or something. All the teachers were middle class and, of course, they were all white. I have some very, very bitter memories of people making me feel like an amoeba. We would know the answers and raise our hands and wouldn't get called on. So we'd sit in back and doodle. I became very angry and very disinterested in school. I wasn't in the main frame because I had been systematically sorted out. I didn't get so angry though that I didn't do my work. I still continued to try and participate. My grades were okay, but I think they could have been better.
>
>One day I decided I was going to chuck it in and I played hookie from school. My parents found out and made me go back. They wouldn't let me quit. But I remember going back angry. I'm still angry, you know! People constantly made me feel like I was not good enough and really assaulted my self-esteem.
>
>After a while, things eased up and I was able to put the smallness of the teachers behind me. I made the honor roll. In my senior year, I was told that I had a very high I.Q. A guidance counselor came around to help us decide what we were going to do after graduation. When he got to me, he blew up. He said, "With your I.Q. you shouldn't have had any grades lower than a 'B' and you shouldn't have had many of those." That was the first time anyone in school recognized my potential.
>
>So because of these negative experiences, I became very internal. I am still not what you call a real social person. I'm mostly around my family, that's my comfort zone, my immediate family.

Siblings and Other Familial Relationships

Besides the relationships that African American girls develop with their parents, there are others that make up the close family network. For economic reasons, the Black family is often an extended family. Grand-parents, aunts, uncles, and other adult relatives may make up the household. These adults would share in the responsibility for child raising.

> My grandmother was ninety-six when she died. I remember her as always being so hard looking. It seemed like she never smiled. When I was about ten years old, these white boys I went to school with started coming over to see me and she'd run them away. I couldn't understand why. She wouldn't even let them up to the door.
>
> So one day, she sat me down and told me about being the daughter of slaves and how for them a white man's interest always meant trouble. My mouth just flew open when Grandma told me about the things that happened. She said, "Work for what you get. Don't ever let nobody give you nothin' and don't accept any special favors. It always means trouble."

Another woman said:

> I was an only child, so my mother and my aunt raised me. My aunt was younger than my mother and I thought she was beautiful. The men thought so too 'cause she always had lots of dates. I used to sit on her bed and watch her dress. She'd tell me about the men she was going out with and let me put on makeup at the same time. She said it was nice to have men friends, but beware of them at the same time. "Never lose your head," she'd say. "Make sure that while you're having fun you keep your smarts about you at the same time."
>
> I really didn't understand all that she was talking about at the time. Now I do (laughter). But I listened to her and when I got older and began to date, I did just what she said. I kept my wits about me, that's what kept me out of trouble I suppose.

Siblings also play an important role in the development of emotional well-being for a Black female. The oldest girl often had a great deal of responsibility and often was in charge of the household while the mother worked.

> I am the daughter of old parents. My father was fifty-six when I was born, and Momma was thirty-eight I guess. Being the baby of eight children had its strong points. Momma always worked, so I was left at home alone a lot. I didn't mind that much though, even now I don't need a lot of people around all the time. I am very comfortable with myself.
>
> Since Momma worked, my two sisters looked out for me a lot. My

oldest sister left home, though, when I was pretty young, so it was actually the sister who is eight years older than I who looked out for me or maybe we looked out for each other. I remember that Momma couldn't tell me about sex, those kinds of things really embarrassed her. So she told me to go ask my sister. I don't think she told me either, I think she just handed me some books to read and told me to come see her if I had any questions. I didn't have any.

When I was about ten years old, I started baby-sitting myself. My five brothers had girlfriends who all had babies and my sister's friends all had children. They'd give me money to take care of all of them. So by the time I got married and had my own children, raising kids was no problem for me. I'd been taking care of kids for years.

Sometimes brothers and sisters did more than just "look out" for one another in the traditional sense. In certain circumstances, brothers and sisters protected each other from real harm when the hardship of oppressive environment erupted in violence.

I ran away from home when I was thirteen years old. I had to. My father was an alcoholic and very abusive. He used to beat me and my brothers and sisters; when he was drunk he would go into this rage and he didn't care what he beat us with. He'd beat my mother, too, she never fought back, she'd just cry.

My mother belonged to this fundamentalist, Pentacostal church. In her faith, the man had the final say. So my father did whatever he wanted and she felt powerless to defend us. Sometimes she would take the beating herself so he would leave us alone, but most of the time he got around to us, too.

I can remember how we used to all huddle together in the next room while he was beating her. We would just hold on to each other crying. Later, Momma would come and hold us, too. She'd rock us and hold us. When I was thirteen, I couldn't take it anymore. I was afraid that if I stayed, he would kill me. So I left. It was survival that motivated me at that point.

I remember standing outside on the corner, shivering and crying. I had nowhere to go, all I knew was that I couldn't go back home. While I was standing there, a man came by and asked me what was wrong. I told him and he told me I could stay with him. I didn't know this man, but I figured he couldn't be any worse than what I left behind. The Lord was looking out for me, cause he wasn't crazy or anything. Later I married him.

After I moved out, my brothers and sisters would come and visit me. My place got to be sort of a hang out, a safe haven. My mother would come, too, sometimes. Now that we are older, my brothers and sisters and I have talked. We decided that even though Momma was too weak to protect us, we always knew she loved us. She didn't want to see us beaten and hurt.

One by one all my brothers and sisters got out after I left. We are all still real close. We check with each other all the time just to see if everything is OK. It's funny we all turned out just fine in spite of the way we grew up.

The African American female, by the time she reaches legal adulthood, has had experiences that make her a woman beyond her years. When the woman who ran away at 13 was asked how she managed as a wife and mother at that young an age, she replied that she really didn't think about it much because she didn't feel that young at the time. Life as a married child was so much better than life as an abused child that she just did what she had to do. When she really got in a bind, she called her mother.

Another woman talked about her relationship with her ex-husband and how she channeled her energy to change a negative experience into a positive one.

I remember my ex-husband told me that I would never amount to anything. He said I'd never have a home, a car, you know all those things that are supposed to spell success. So, I just love the old "prove them wrong" theory. When people tell me you won't amount to anything, you won't do anything, or you won't have anything, I just work that much harder to be a success. I remember when I got my first car I drove past my ex-husband's house and blew the horn and waved! But that's how I look at everything now, even in my work. I don't let people put me down. Now when I think about it, I don't think I'm trying to prove that they're wrong, I'm proving that I am right.

Black Women as Sisters

Even as Black women learn to accept extra responsibility, there is a place for fun and laughter so that they don't break under the weight of it all. Often the release from stress is found with friends. Strong friendship and kinship relationships are an important part of the extended family relationship. Families grew accustomed to having "extra" people around. "Momma always fixed a few extra plates because she never knew which one of us was bringing a friend home to eat."

Several of the women in this study were raised in an environment where their mother's friends played a very substantial role in their

upbringing. These women or "aunts" could often relate to them in ways
their mother could not.

> When I was fifteen years old, my mother and I fell out. I don't even
> remember what it was all about now. But I was mad. So I decided that
> I'd get even and run away. I packed up my bag and went over to my god-
> mother's house. She was so glad to see me. She told me to come right
> on in. We had a ball. I let her cook for me and she cooked all my favorite
> food. She even sent her husband out for the things they didn't have on
> hand (laughter).
> I stayed there for a few days, then I started getting worried when
> nobody from home called for me or came by. What, didn't they miss me?
> What kind of parents did I have? I didn't know that she had called
> mother almost as soon as I got there and told her I was safe, so don't
> worry. I went home, I think, that weekend. Mother acted like nothing
> happened. I don't think I ran away anymore after that.

Having a friend who could be trusted to care for a child was a relief
for many Black mothers who, between work and household chores, had
little time for themselves. But close friendships were also helpful in
relieving the stress of day-to-day life.

> I grew up listening to what I call "women talk." My mother's friends
> would come by or she would talk to them on the phone. They would just
> laugh. My mother always seemed different when she was talking to her
> friends, younger and more relaxed.

These women were later to develop close friendships of their own
and would come to rely upon their relationships with their friends. It
is often difficult to determine when a Black female is speaking of a sister, aunt, or cousin if they are really related or not. But as one woman
said, "It doesn't really matter; it takes a lot more than blood to make a
family."

> I met my best friend when I was in third grade. She saved me from
> starving to death. This was during the Depression and since there were
> so many of us, we fixed anything we could get our hands on for lunch.
> Peanut butter and jelly was standard. Sometimes you just slam two
> pieces of bread together, this was a "jam sandwich" (laughter). But the
> other girl's father kept his job during the depression and she and her
> sister had the best. She would come to school with nice ham sandwiches
> or tuna sandwiches. Things we couldn't afford and she would give them

to me. She didn't want them. So we'd trade sandwiches. When she moved away the next year, I really missed her.

But we moved a few years later; and when I went to my new school and I walked in my room, there she was! I started to grin and so did she. She remembered me, too! We were always together after that. The thing I appreciated most about her was that she would listen. She wasn't much of a talker, you know, she'd say a few things. But I could trust that when I told her something, it wouldn't go any farther. A secret was safe with her.

At another level, African American women are able to relate to one another as sisters in the struggle. They are aware of the difficulties they face in trying to "make it."

> The Black woman who is on the lowest economic, status and prestige rung, barely surviving and not knowing from time to time how she will provide for her children or herself, and her Black sister (who because of "relative" opportunity, education or luck has been able to be upwardly mobile within the allowed limitations) are inextricably linked by their common oppression whether it takes the form of the overt daily hassle of the street or the covert sugar-coated arsenic of higher education. The sister struggling to feed her family and the sister of more fortunate economic circumstance (no matter how hostile they may be to each other at one level) know that on the other level, they have both been called "Black bitch" with equal venom.[152]

As long as institutional racism and sexism exists in this country, the African American woman realizes that at any given time the doors of opportunity can slam in her face. She will be confronted time and time again with her color. Often the slights are subtle, but they sting no less painfully. "Where I work, I am the only Black woman. The other women go to lunch together everyday, they wait for each other, but they never ask me. What do they think, I like eating alone?"

Whether it is being excluded from little social engagements or being passed over for an assignment, the Black woman has to learn how to cope in these situations, how to handle herself, and, if necessary, how to fight given the opportunity. In her vulnerability to racist or sexist attack, the seemingly successful Black woman is much like her less fortunate sister who has probably had to learn to cope as well, but often with a lot less.

Often when faced with a situation of isolation, Black women find themselves drawn together in support of one another. As one woman put it, "Hey, we keep each other going; me I'm going to always help another 'sister' out." The fact that there is still a need for Black associations, organizations, and schools is indicative of the still smoldering racial attitudes that underlie the social, economic, and political climate of this nation.

Deep Spiritual Awareness

> How I got over, over
> my soul looks back in
> wonder of how I got over.
> – Traditional Negro spiritual

The words to this song and many more like it can be heard Sunday after Sunday as churches in the Black community fill with the Black faithful.

> I personally don't like going to church on Sunday and staying for three
> or four hours, but I'm like most Black people, you're going to find me
> in church on Sunday. That's because we know that has been our source
> . . . that's one thing we have in common, we know what the Lord can
> do for us.

Religious faith is probably the one thing that unites African American people with their African roots. Although most of the slaves who were brought to America were forced into Christianity, there was already a religious, a spiritual base on which this faith was built. "Indeed the African man lived in a 'religious universe' and this meant that all his activities were experienced with religious meaning and significance."[153] African traditional religions were the primary form of worship in most of the Western African nations, though Islamic and Christian influences were not uncommon.

With the slave trade, the white landowners were faced with a dilemma. It went against their "Christian" nature, on the one hand, to enslave fellow Christians. Yet on the other hand, there was a need to strip the Africans of all of the vestiges of home and that meant their gods and their faith as well. So under the pretense of "saving the heathens," Black Africans were stripped of their African names, given "Christian" names, and stripped of their native gods and given a new white god.

The outcome of this conversion was not foreseen, for the one thing that the Africans understood was religion.

Thus the slave transformed Christianity and reinterpreted the Scriptures in the light of the black religious experience. He was not led to an understanding of God via the Scriptures; rather, the deepest meanings of the Scriptures themselves were interpreted in the light of the slave's African religious background, his situation of despair, and his personal meeting with God.[154]

In this manner, the act that was meant to take away the African people's last link with home and insure their subjugation was the act that was eventually to set them free. The Black church, more than any other institution, has been the place where freedom has been acted out. The church is a binding place where Black people come together to share in their faith and heal each other's wounds.

Those who have been critical of the faith, who have accused Black people of having a "pie in the sky" religious fanaticism, do not understand the nature of Black religion or the relationship that Black people have with God.

Black religion presupposes a God who identifies in a personal way with Black people in a society where such a human relationship is uncommon ... the notion is, "if God is for you, who can be against you?" And there is a second question as well, "if God is for you, must you not be for yourselves?"[155]

So the slaves prayed and at the same time the foundation for freedom was laid. Even the songs of the spirituals took on special meaning as those who were strong hearted planned to "steal away home."

While it is true that religion can be an opiate and keep people from acting in their own behalf, "when a Black mother tells you she's praying for you you'd better watch out, there is power in those words. Something's going to happen and if it wasn't going to happen, she'll make it happen!"

James Cone gives a wonderful answer to those who criticize the eschatological nature of Black religious faith. He states that, yes, there is a certain element of eschatology, but those who criticize don't understand that this *is* the source of power.

If there is a realm of reality that is eschatological, then evil and suffering do not have the last word. For what is, is also coming to be. This was precisely the message of the Black spirituals and of Black religion generally. Because Black slaves believed that what is was coming to be, they refused to let their humanity be defined by the historical limitations of slavery. . . . For hope in Black religion is based on a vision *not* present in, but created out of historical struggle. If we limit our hope to what is, then we destroy hope. Hope is the expectation of that which is not. It is the belief that the impossible is possible, the "not yet" is coming in history. Hope is what enabled Frederick Douglass, Harriett Tubman, Rosa Parks, and Martin Luther King to actualize historical projects of freedom which others said were impossible.[156]

Black women are and have been the mainstays of the church. Though the fundamentalist traditions of the major African American congregations have kept women out of the pulpit and other leadership roles until recently, they still fill the pews on Sundays. Even those who are not really actively involved in church still feel connected, if for no other reason than that they had to go when they were a child. They may stay away from the church building, but the faith dies much harder.

My mother always kept us in church and I loved going to church because that is where you get your spiritual guidance, your spiritual heading, but since I was sixteen I haven't been in church. . . . [M]y kids don't go to church, sorry to say. They need to go to church, but I do have Bibles over the bed and we have Bible stores that they read.

Most of the women who were interviewed for this study still had strong ties to the church and thought of the church as yet another extension of family. Like their African forefathers and foremothers, they found it difficult to separate their religious beliefs from the way they tried to live their lives. Being truly Christian was difficult sometimes, but as one woman said, "God ain't through with me yet."

It was interesting for these women to reflect, to get their "souls to look back," and remember when the words that they heard every Sunday rang true in their lives.

My husband had returned from military service and, I don't know, he just couldn't handle it. He wasn't used to being part of the household and he wanted to know everything that was going on, everything that I was doing. And the kids and I weren't used to anyone asking. There was a lot of tension as he tried to exert this macho image. So it happened one day, he snapped. One night he just started shooting up the house. Of course, I was trying to protect the children and I got shot, but in that moment I did not worry because I felt protected. I knew whatever he did I was going to be okay.

I was hurt really bad. I didn't fully recover for a long time. But I knew that I would, I just felt it. And I have never held it against my husband for what he did. He had a breakdown and when he told me he was sorry, I believed him. He just couldn't deal with returning home and being part of a household tha really functioned well without him and he snapped. So I don't hold any bitterness. We are not together, but if something were to happen and he needed me to help, I'd help him, after all he's the father of my children.

Since that day I've known that I can make it. I truly believe that there's nothing I can't do with the help of God. And I don't even look back, I just keep on going.

Another woman said:

I early decided that I wanted to serve God, don't ask me where that came from, I would say the spirit, but now when I think about it, I had gone to Catholic school and I liked the nuns, they were friendly, they related to me. I was a good student in school so they allowed me to get to know them more as people (of course, now I know that they thought I was okay, I was an exception, you know). But, as a child, I felt I wanted to be a sister. But I didn't get much farther than that at the time. My remarks were met with more or less ambivalence. A black nun was unheard of.

It didn't come up again until I was about a senior in high school. I heard a sermon on the actual grace and awareness is the promise of the Holy Spirit. I was sitting there saying to myself, "How do you know that your desire to become a sister is not one of the promises of the Holy Spirit?" And running through my mind was, "If I don't try it in terms of sisterhood, will I regret that I should have or could have and ought to have later on in life?"

So off I went to the convent . . . [and] during those years of hardship, I was still growing in grace with the Lord. In the prayers we said everyday, I certainly felt accepted by the Lord, affirmed by the Lord, and affirmed in terms that what I was doing was what the Lord wanted me to do. So even though all of this craziness was going on around me at all levels, there was a communion going on; and I was hearing the Scriptures and hearing the Psalms. I would say that is the secret of my "success," my belief and my faith and my active relationship with the Lord.

The belief that a relationship with God should be an active rather than passive experience is a far cry from a "pie in the sky" relationship. As James Cone said, "I do not remember any black church person using religion to cover up oppression or as an escape from the harsh realities of life."[157] In fact, it was their religion that inspired them. For out of religious faith, they realized that "freedom is not a gift, but a responsibility, and thus must be taken against the will of those who hold us in bondage."[158]

An active relationship with God is often maintained by prayer. Prayer in the Black tradition takes on many forms, however. It is viewed more as a "talking with" God and is often free verse rather than formalized prayers. This woman talks about prayer and how it became an important part of her life.

> It wasn't until maybe five or six years ago that I realized that I can be driving down the street and talk to Him like I'm talking to you and He would hear my prayer. I was like everyone else I guess. When I was younger, I thought you had to get on your knees, and say "Lord, you gotta help me" and the Lord would hear your prayer. Then I realized that I didn't have to wait until something happened to talk to Him. I could just talk whenever I felt like it. I could say, "Lord, thank you for waking me up today." That was a prayer. And so I talked to a friend about it. And I said, "Teach me how to pray." And he said, "You've already got it. What do you think you're doing when you sing all of those songs?" [She sings in a gospel ensemble.] He said, "I don't need to teach you how to pray." I thought about it, and I said, "Well, I am praying." Sometimes it just takes somebody else to make you realize that you're already doing what you set out to do.

Black Community Connectedness

Very closely linked to the African American woman's strong relationship to the church is her relationship to the whole Black community. This is probably in part due to the fact that the church has long been the focus of Black community activity.

The Black community is generally characterized by a "quality of spontaneity, openness to feelings, and emotional vitality. People are expected to be for real, down-to-earth, authentic and genuine."[159] The people act and interact within this community environment, sharing their joys and sorrow.

Black females are often drawn together in support networks within their own communities. They look after each other's children and supply each other with needed information.

Cooperation rather than competition has proven to be an important factor in the African American struggle for freedom. Especially in years past, Blacks who succeeded were very conscious that a victory for one person was a victory for all. The achievements of Black heroes and heroines are lifted up as inspiration for all.

> Somewhere along the line, I guess I began to wonder why it always seemed that the only thing I ever saw about black people was derogatory. I thought, why is this when I knew better, I knew good things were going on. So I got interested in Black history and I took a class. It was the only class that really perked me up. For example, ... I'd be sitting in a regular history class, it was usually dull, the teacher would be talking about Christopher Columbus as they always did. But in Black history, we'd talk about George Washington Carver and my mind would say, "Wake up!" I wanted to know more about these people and their contributions.
>
> I realized later when I began teaching that the history books didn't include black people because people didn't want you to know about them. If you didn't know what your people had done and had accomplished, then you would never feel that you could do anything, you see.
>
> So I think my main inspiration was finding out about the black heroes and heroines. By reading about Mary McCleod-Bethune and how she started a college with five little girls in one little room with five orange crates for desks, then I thought maybe I can do that, too.

In the African American context, the family and the community are seen as the basic unit, not the individual. The uniqueness of each individual is acknowledged, but an individual's unique gifts were given to be shared with all.

> I trace my success back to my parents, back to a family unit that came from the South. They knew themselves as Black people in a racist society and yet they were in a way nurtured because they were in a segregated Black community. Because of that, they were very learned in Black history and had Black values.
>
> My parents had a thing about us developing ourselves to the best of our ability and developing skills, being college educated – and all of that was for service to the community.

The Black orientation toward collective survival is another remnant of past African traditions. To view all life as interrelated is part of the African world view. The African mindset believes in the connectedness of the whole universe arranged in a hierarchy that includes God, humans, animals, plants, and inanimate objects in descending order.[160] While much has been lost because of the influences of an imposed Euro-American culture, there is still a tendency for Black people to believe that we are all "in this thing together." When the civil rights of one Black person are denied, then the civil rights of all African Americans stand in jeopardy.

All Black women stand to fall when one sister falls beneath the blows of institutionalized racism and sexism or when she is forced to raise her family on a marginal income in substandard conditions because the promise that Thomas Jefferson gave to America of "life, liberty, and the pursuit of happiness" was never meant to include the sons and daughters of the African slave. The stereotypes that are placed on the head of one are used to denounce us all.

> I love my job. I love helping people, helping kids. I have over six hundred people, volunteers, on this side of town that depend on me. They say people in CHA are lazy; they don't want to do nothing. That's bull.
>
> I love helping people feel better about themselves. Two of the women [I had worked with] came back to me and told me they had done what I told them to do and it worked. They wanted to thank me. I told them, "Don't thank me, just continue what you're doing and make me proud. That's thanks enough. You don't have to give me nothing, just make me proud of you, be proud of yourself, make your kids proud of you."

Chapter 5

The Will of the African American Woman: An Interpretation

> She impressed me as a woman of marked individuality and strong character. She was no reed shaken by the wind. She did her own thinking; had opinions of her own, and held to them with great tenacity.... [T]here was also combined in her a heart as tender as that of a child. How wonderfully sympathetic she was; how readily did she enter into the sorrows, the heartaches of others, how natural it seemed for her to take up all who needed to be soothed and comforted.
>
> —Eulogy for Harriet Jacobs, given by the
> Reverend Francis Grimke, March 1987[161]

The above was written for one woman, Harriet Jacobs, who was born a slave. Her eulogy, however, speaks for many Black women. Their eulogies may never appear in a book, but they will be remembered in the hearts of those who they touched and inspired along the way.

To understand the meaning of what it means to be a self-willed African American woman, one cannot rely solely on theories and concepts which are framed in a Euro-American mindset, based on Western beliefs, and measured in terms of a value system which has suppressed and subjugated both minorities and women. To understand the will of a Black woman, one must look at her life and how her relationships and beliefs serve as a reference point for all that she does.

In Chapter 1, the basic argument on the nature of the human will was outlined and key concepts constituting essential elements in the debate on human will were identified. "Freedom," "power," and "self-determination" are terms used frequently in traditional discussions of self-will. They will now be examined again in the context of the life of the African American woman.

Power and the African American Woman

Power in an African American context has to do with relationships: the relationship with ourselves; the relationship with God; and the relationship with family, friends, and community, all bring power. For it is within these relationships that we feel comfortable to act and to express ourselves, knowing that we will be affirmed for who and what we are. As an individual, each woman possesses unique talents; but it is only within a relationship that these talents are affirmed. As one woman said, "My whole approach to life is much more community oriented than it is individualist, that obviously comes from the way my parents raised me. I certainly have my private times, but I'm thirsty for relationships."

In the novel *Sula*, Eva Peace had power. Physically confined to a wheelchair, her room was the center of activity; people were drawn to her. Her power came from her easy nature and her ability to put people at ease. She did not control the people around her; they were allowed to be whatever they wanted to be.

There are limits to what individuals can do. While a single act can make a difference, it is when one person's act sparks others to act that the whole world changes. Power has given Black people the ability to maintain integrity in the face of injustice and to never compromise one's beliefs for the sake of expediency.

If a person uses power to enslave and oppress another person, then both individuals are oppressed – the slaves because they are controlled by the oppressor and the oppressors because they are controlled by their need to oppress. When any one person controls all of the power, it corrupts. Power is to be shared by all, for the good of all.

This understanding of shared power comes not only from a world view influenced by African values and frame of reference, it also comes from the Black Christian tradition and their interpretation of the Scriptures. For Black people, God, who is all powerful, gives people power so they can work for Him. As one woman said,

> Now you know God could have freed the Israelites all by Himself, don't you? But He didn't do that. He gave a little power to Moses and together they set the people free. Now if God doesn't hog all the power, what makes people come along and think they should?

Self-Determination and the African American Woman

The Black female ability to define herself comes from a belief that no human has the right to define another. Each person is a unique creation of God; and with God, the individual elicits her own becoming. An old saying from the Black tradition shares the wisdom that there are only two things that everyone born must do: The first one is that we all must die, and the second is that we all must live until we die. What one does between birth and death is up to each individual and their God to work out.

The Black female who understands this knows that only she has the responsibility to determine her path. The Black woman knows that she is constantly in a state of becoming as she reconnects with God, family, and community, and as she is moved in different directions. Women like Maya Angelou are not opposed to taking risks and extending themselves for they know that failure only comes from not trying. "Resilience and revitalization of the human spirit are facilitated by the use of humor and the knowledge that one is not alone."[162] If she succeeds, then she was true to herself and what she wanted and felt she could become.

Zora Neale Hurston died penniless; but she lived a full, rich life. She was not concerned with what others thought of her; she was herself and always "proud to be, colored me."

Freedom and African American Women

In *Their Eyes Were Watching God,* Janie Starks found freedom in a relationship with a man where she was treated as an equal partner. Tea Cake Woods did not have money or prestige, but with him Janie was able to grow into a woman in her own right. She was not a pretty possession to be seen but not heard.

In Alice Walker's novel, *The Color Purple,* in the friendship that developed between Shug and Celie, both women found a space for freedom. Celie was able to recognize her inner beauty that had long been suppressed, and Shug was freed from her own vanity. Her vanity allowed Shug to move into Celie's house and sleep with Celie's husband. Freed, she could sense Celie's pain and she worked to end it.

Freedom is what we constantly struggle for, yet absolute freedom is never attained. Freedom in the African American context is far from the ability to do as one wants. It is not a "state of nature," for in nature the rule is one of survival. Humans have been given the ability to exist, not merely as animals, but as animals who have the ability to coexist with one another.

When human freedom is attained, individuals will be able to coexist as a human family. In the African mindset, the universe, God, humans, and all of nature are linked. The riches of the earth are for all to share. Each person must contribute for the good of all. In the Scriptures, Cain asked God, "Am I my brother's keeper?" From the African perspective, the answer would be a resounding "Yes!" We are all keepers for ourselves and for each other.

Remnants of that world view remain in the traditional values of the Black community. It becomes difficult in the face of growing materialism to hold on to values that place people above property. It is not what you have that determines who you are; you can be bound in chains and yet your soul can remain free.

To the extent that we as human beings can continuously struggle to "bridge the gap between what we are and what we desire to be, and then in making an intentional effort to cross the gap, knowing the only alternative is staying where we are, that we feel provisionally free."[163]

Self-Will and the African American Woman

Self-will has been defined in terms of power, self-determination, and freedom. It relates to the amount of power we have as humans to determine a course of action and then act on it. Self-will also relates to how we see ourselves and how others see us. By exercising our will, we move closer to becoming the person we want ourselves to be. It is a self-creating process as we forever move from what is to what is to be.

From an African American perspective, all of the above is true. However, more importantly, for Black females, the will is where that which is human and that which is spiritual meet. The strength of Black women comes from the knowledge that above all else we have the power to be in a relationship with God and then to act with God in the creation of the world to come. "With this faith we will be able to work together, to pray together, to struggle together, to stand up for freedom together, knowing that we will be free one day" – Dr. Martin Luther King, Jr.[164]

A Portrait of the Self-Willed Black Woman

The strong-willed Black woman may come from a single parent family or from a family where both parents were present. Her interactions and relationships probably extended far beyond her "nuclear" faily. She was probably scolded by grandparents, aunts, godparents, and family friends. She probably played with sisters, brothers, cousins, and neighbors.

She may come from the middle class with many material comforts or she may have grown up in public housing where comforts were few, but the outer environment was never considered as important as the inner environment. Humor was plentiful, and family mealtimes were turned into joyous occasions where family members processed the day's events. Pain was shared too, no matter whether it was a temporary sorrow or a heartbreaking tragedy. Slights, disappointments, problems, and defeats were all brought to the table and shared. These were processed within the family. If one family member was hurting, everyone was concerned and everyone worked together to plan a suitable course of action.

No matter where she lived or grew up this woman was probably privy to the same conventional wisdom that has been passed down in Black households from one generation to the next. Some adult, usually the mother or grandmother, probably said to her:

"The truth will out."
"God don't like ugly."
"Hard head makes a soft behind."
"One monkey don't stop no show."
"If you lay down with dogs you gonna come up with fleas."
"What goes around comes around."
"You don't git old being no fool."

These are just a few of the sayings that African American women, who are not adults, can relate to. They were used frequently as mini-lessons to teach that common sense or "mother wit" was every bit as important as anything she would learn in school. In fact, it was a bitter admonishment when a girl was said to be "full of book learning, but ain't got a lick of sense."

The strong-willed Black woman more than likely spent a great deal of time with her mother. In the shadow of her mother, she learned how to "take care of business." She learned that she could only expect to get out of life what she put into it and "ain't nothing worth having free." Knowing this, she was not afraid to work hard for what she wanted and she grew in confidence as she saw her small efforts pay off.

When she went to school, she knew she must work hard there, too. She had to do the best that she could. Education is important and school is no place to play. "You learn all that you can. You'll need it to get ahead."

She learned about her personal heroes and heroines, African

Americans and even members of her own family who somehow made a difference. These are the people she would never read about in the history books at school. She learned these things at home. There was one history at school, but it was at home she learns about herself. Passed down word of mouth, the Black girl learned about the people she came from.

This woman also probably went to church on Sunday, where she learned that for Black people, "God has made a way out of no way." She learned of the struggle of her people and how she must continue to press on, always reaching out to the people who need her and reaching up to God.

> I'm still working my life out with the Lord. I don't want anybody to follow me. I think the best thing that I can do is help a person learn how to follow that spirit and recognize their gifts and discover who they are. I'm still struggling, so I don't want anyone else to be like me. I want people to discover for themselves that like the song says, "Your momma may have and your papa may have, but God bless the child that has her own."

Conclusions

> Negroes have no control over their education and have little voice in their other affairs pertaining thereto. In a few cases Negroes have been chosen as members of public boards of education, and some have been appointed members of private boards, but these Negroes are always such a small minority that they do not figure in the final working out of the educational program. The education of the Negroes, then, the most important thing in the uplift of the Negroes, is almost entirely in the hands of those who have enslaved them and now segregate them.
>
> —Carter G. Woodson[165]

Although Carter G. Woodson wrote this indictment against American education and the treatment of African Americans over 60 years ago, with the exception to the reference to racial segregation, the same statement could be written about American education today. African Americans still have little control over what they learn and the way they learn it. A few more African Americans head school boards, supervise school districts and participate in education decision-making. Yet they still figure "only in a small way to the final working of the educational program."[166]

American education has always assumed that a relevant education is one which reflects the interests, the values, and the potentials of the white middle class. And since Blacks and their interests are generally excluded from serious recognition in the conventional American universe of significant values, American education must be considered a way our [Black] society is organized and maintained. In consequence, the low self-estimate of Black Americans dictated by their prescribed place in the body politic, is continually reinforced and encouraged by our systems of education.[167]

Adult education shares in this indictment. In its attention to inclusiveness, adult education rates no better than the general American system. Adult education theory and practice reflect the "values, interests, and potentials" of the dominant culture and the African American has virtually been ignored in research agendas. As adult educators continue to develop "adult learning theories," they do not mention that these "theories" are really culture specific and, therefore, may not serve all adults. When these theories are then put into practice on people different from those for whom they were designed, the people are claimed to be the failures, not the theories.

Until it is acknowledged that adult education research agendas have been culturally and racially biased and a conscious effort is made to develop program models based on theories generated for and sometimes by the people they serve, then those who have continually been marginalized in this society will continue to be victims of miseducation.

Implications for Research

Much more research needs to be done which relates specifically to African American adult education. There are few historical references to African Americans and their efforts in adult education despite the fact it has been recorded that during and after slavery African Americans have struggled to educate themselves. Education has been directly linked to the struggle for freedom. The Freedom Schools and the historically black universities and colleges are testimonies to the African Americans' thirst for knowledge.

Research that focuses on African American learning styles, as well as cognitive and psychological development, is also needed. It should not be assumed that the developmental phases for all adults are the same. The fact that so many theories of development derived from within the dominant culture alone suggests that this could not possibly be true.

Since the African American framework is clearly inspired by a world view that is more African than it is European, one should expect some differences in the way African American development occurs. Research which contributes to the development of theoretical perspectives that move away from European models and which takes on models more relevant to Afrocentric perspectives and beliefs will be unique contributions to this growing field.

This would seem to suggest that more research that is participatory and phenomenological in nature should be encouraged. African American culture values cooperation and interdependence. Present research models, even those that engage the researcher as participant observer, impose theory on people rather than allowing them to participate in building it. It is also presumptuous for academics to assume that only they have the faculties or perspectives to produce a rigorous study.

This research focused solely on African American females and the emergence of will. Similar investigations relating to African American males would help us all to judge whether the same factors which influence Black females play the same roles in the lives of Black males.

The Black male has been frequently frustrated in his attempt to live up to the American model of father-provider. For this reason tension has developed between Black females and males which if allowed to go unanalyzed may drive more and more Black men out of the home. This, in turn, will probably contribute to the further decline of the Black community and will ensure more Black women and Black children live in poverty.

Implications for Adult Education Theory

Present adult education theory reflects the research agendas that have been supported by the dominant communities. Adult education is a broad field, and whereas research based on issues of concern to those of the dominant culture is necessary, much more attention must be paid to the development of theories which also help those marginalized populations who must rely on this nation's dominant public systems along very broad social and educational spectrums.

Adult education was first institutionalized in the United States as a means to guarantee that U.S. citizens would have the skills and knowledge to participate in this democracy. An educated citizenry was seen as vital to the survival and well-being of this nation. What is to happen to this nation now, when more and more citizens are being excluded from its processes?

Self-directedness and perspective transformation are important concepts for those who are engaging in educational pursuits for personal advancement or enrichment. But also remember that there is a different cultural context that values relationships and social commitment over individual achievement. Adult education theory must also reflect some of these other voices.

Implications for Practice

Programs designed for women in the African American community should reflect an African American value system.

1. They should be interactive and noncompetitive.
2. They should be holistic in nature, focusing on the students' feelings and emotional well-being as well as skill attainment.
3. Programs should make use of structures and networks already in place within the community such as churches, community groups, and fraternal organizations.
4. Teachers should be realistic role models and mentors for the students. While it is not always important that the teachers are black, white teachers should be sensitive and appreciative of cultural differences.
5. Innovative, intergenerational educational models could also be developed. Mother and daughter programs might prove to be very successful because these programs would draw upon a solid relationship. Mothers and daughters often work together and share family responsibilities; working together on educational projects could prove rewarding for both.

The African American woman is like a magnet. She draws people to her, she connects with others and from them gains strength and determination. Most of all, adult education programs should provide the African American woman with a solid base of connections and affirm the person she is, freeing her to open up and become.

Appendix A:
Themes of Self-Will

Four themes were considered essential structures in the development of a strong, self-determined Black female. These themes were family relationships, especially the mother-daughter bond; Black women as sisters; deep spiritual awareness; and Black community connectedness.

Black Family Relationships —
The Mother-Daughter Bond

Black women have a particularly strong relationship with their mothers. This relationship is often based on interdependence, with the daughters taking on early responsibility and helping her mother with daily family needs.

Linda

I am a strong, Black woman because I was raised by a strong Black woman. One of those so-called determined Black women. It is a known fact that when a Black woman is determined, watch out. Nothing is going to keep her back. So, just seeing her and watching her made me want to be as strong as she was, if not stronger.

Ellie

When I was young, my mother and father started having some difficulties. My father decided that he was going to withdraw funds from the family. My mother went to work at . . . I'll never forget, a raincoat factory, during the war. She was a piece worker. She'd come home at night, dead tired and together we'd figure out how much she had earned for the day. I started to look at her, how she reacted to things and how she carried herself. It was as if the whole time she was saying, "Hey, I'm keeping my family together, I will do what I have to do." So just to see what Momma was doing, working and standing on her own, not in some subservient role, it was very different. I started to tie into what my Momma was doing because it seemed she had a good thing going.

Later, same interview:

I decided to work full time and go to school part time so that I could help Momma. I did. We had a very good life and she had the last laugh in the end anyway. My mother died about twenty years ago and she left Daddy a dollar, okay. He has yet to get over that.

Lisa

My mother had initiative, creativity. She could just do things. I mean there were times when we would paint the house and she kept an immaculate house. I mean we had carpeting, we had a whole bunch of things that other people in the neighborhood just didn't have in two parent families.

Connie

On the whole, I would say that my mother was the strong one. That's the truth, it was my Momma. That's funny. It looks like she was the one who always was doing everything. She was right there whenever something was going on.

Fannie

I think most black women, well myself, I think I get all my strengths all hidden powers from my mother. I started from a little girl up. My mother had thirteen children, and I have seen my mother give birth to two of my sisters and brothers one day and the next day she was back at her job.

Besides stressing hard work, Black mothers encouraged their daughters to work hard in school. Education is seen as crucial to future success and achievement.

Lou

Education was everything to my mother, you see she didn't have it. My mother probably went to eighth grade, I don't think Daddy even got that far. But all eight of my mother's children graduated from high school. Two of us went to college, my sister finally finished college, she went back. I never did. I really didn't like school that much.

Maggie

I was an excellent student because my mother had been the teacher in this one room school down South and so she taught us. She had us interested in reading. I remember one incident, I guess I was in first grade. The teacher had us up to the black board to teach us how to write our ABCs. She put up a big "A" and said everybody make an "A." Well, my mother had already taught me my ABCs so I started writing. I was all the way to "F" before the teacher stopped me. She said, "You stand in the corner," and she put a dunce cap on my head. It was a long time before I understood why I was being punished. Of course, all of those teachers were white, no doubt racist too, and they wanted to discourage the Black students. That sort of disillusioned me. Fortunately for many kids that experience might have left a lasting imprint on them, discouraging them, but apparently it didn't do that to me because I didn't let it phase me. I just kept on learning.

Fannie

When it comes to education, I don't even have to deal with that. My husband stays on them about that. He tells them that education is the only way out.

Tonia

I did graduate from high school and I promised my mother that I would get some type of degree. When my daughter was 13, I decided to go back to school and I went back to school and I received my bachelor's degree in social work.

Annie

I couldn't have gone through law school without my mother's help. We had a place together, so that took care of the childcare for my daughter. I mean she was really there for me. She is still very supportive of me and my daughter.

Betty

Now I have to be strong. My daughter, Joyce, is in medical school. She wants to be a doctor, so you know I've got to help her all I can.

Sometimes a mother's love can be tough too since Black mothers feel obligated to prepare their daughters for the obstacles they will encounter.

Tonia

I got pregnant with my daughter my senior year of high school and I was unable to take the track scholarship I had received. So when I graduated, I immediately went into the work force; I had to get a job. I did graduate from high school; I had promised my mother I would get my diploma. But I was really upset with my mother. I wanted to go to college. I felt I had an opportunity and she should take responsibility and raise my child. I was angry with everyone. Now I thank my mother because I feel if she had let me do what I wanted to do, I wouldn't be the person I am today.

Jane

I went to work after my daughter was born. Sometimes I didn't want to, but my mother influenced me by telling me, "Hey, this is your kid, this is your responsibility. You were grown enough to make this baby, blah, blah, you know." So I did and it wasn't that bad.

Later, same interview:

We have a strong, matriarchal thread in my family. You talk about getting in trouble, not going to jail, not doing dope and it was all because we didn't want Granny to learn. No one wanted Granny to find out. So that was a very strong influence.

Fannie

If you really love your child, then it's up to you to provide for that child and for that child's future and you have to be strong, you have to look out for the child.

Lou

I raised my four children; I did it. Their father helped because he worked and provided well for us and that enabled me to stay at home and raise my children. But I see myself in all that they do. It makes me feel good when my friends, and sometimes people I don't know, tell me what wonderful children I have. I know I have good children, but it wasn't easy. It took a whole lot of cussing and a whole lot of praying.

The Role of the Father

Fathers were also important in the upbringing of children. They often shared responsibility with the mothers in preparing children to confront racism and other social barriers.

Sister Joan

The main barrier, of course, for me has been racism, but my parents started militating against that early. We always ate supper together and after supper we would sit around and talk about what had happened during the day. We would analyze it. Of course, that's not the language they used, but that's what we did. And my father would say something like two wrongs don't make a right, and we would discuss how we could go back in there and do battle. So we were trained not to let those things that occurred get to us. We processed that in our family and figured out how we could get around and cope despite the social barriers that were there. We learned to make a "way out of no way."

Connie

My Dad used to always tell me, you can do whatever you want to do, if you really want to do it. So if you are going to be a bum, be a good bum. If you are going to be a bag lady, be a good bag lady. He also told me to be independent, not to sit around and wait for somebody to do something for you when you could do it yourself.

Later, same interview:

I talked to my father about everything. My mother, I didn't talk to her as much, we're friends, but I didn't talk to her as much. I always felt she had eight other kids that she had to deal with so I would never take her my problems. I took my problems to my Daddy, so when he died it was like, well the end, that's all.

Tonia

My father died when I was seven years old, but today, even now I still talk to him. If I have a problem I'll talk to my father about it. I know he hears me, wherever he is, and I feel comforted.

Jane

From early childhood, my parents talked to both my brother and I about being the best you could be. Showing people what you were all about. When I went to these integrated schools, you know people had all of the stereotypes: all Negroes were stupid, we acted like animals, you know, all the old clichés. I think I decided that it only took a little more effort. I had to prove them wrong, and maybe it's not to prove them wrong, but it's to prove me right. You know, a positive affirmation.

Other Familial Relationships

Connie

My grandmother was ninety-six when she died. I remember her as always being so hard looking. She never smiled. When I was about ten years old these white boys I went to school with started coming over to see me and she'd run them away. I couldn't understand why. She wouldn't even let them up to the door.

So one day she sat me down and told me about being the daughter of slaves and how for them a white man's interest meant trouble. My mouth just flew open when Grandma told me about the things that happened. She said, "Work for what you get. Don't ever let nobody give you nothin' and don't accept any special favors. It always means trouble."

Jane

You know as you get older, you kind of want something on that tombstone . . . in that "obit.," you know (laughter). I want to impress my family. I want to impress upon my daughter that she can accomplish things. . . . I guess I have to try to do as much as possible because I do have family, I do have people who care and I have to get from yesterday to tomorrow.

Lou

I am the daughter of old parents. My father was fifty-six when I was born and Momma was about thirty-eight, I guess. Being the baby of eight children had its strong points. Momma always worked so I was left at home alone a lot. I didn't mind that much though. Even now I don't need a lot of people around all the time. I am very comfortable with myself.

Since Momma worked, my two sisters looked out for me a lot. My oldest sister left home though when I was pretty young, so it was actually the sister who is eight years older than I who looked out for me or maybe we looked out for each other. I remember that Momma couldn't tell me about sex, those kinds of things really embarrassed her. So she told me to go ask my sister. I don't think she told me either, I think she just handed me some books to read and told me to come see her if I had any questions. I didn't have any.

When I was about ten years old I started babysitting myself. My five brothers and girlfriends who all had babies and my sister's friends all had chidren. They'd give me money to take care of all of them. So by the time I got married and had my own children, raising kids was no problem for me. I'd been taking care of kids for years.

Mary

I still don't want to embarrass my family, my children and my grandchildren. I want to make some kind of valuable contribution, you know. Some of the contributions may be small, but then you never know how seeds grow ... as long as I have encouragement from some people, a little pat on the back, hey, that keeps me going. And you stop to think, well, maybe I can bring somebody else along. It perpetuates the feeling that is within this family and within this group.

Tia

I ran away from home when I was thirteen years old. I had to. My father was an alcoholic and very abusive. He used to beat me and my brothers and sisters; when he got drunk, he'd go into this rage and he didn't care what he beat us with. He'd beat my mother, too. She never fought back, she'd just cry.

My mother belonged to this fundamentalist Pentecostal church. In her faith, the man had the final say. So my father did whatever he wanted and she felt powerless to defend us. Sometimes she would take the beating herself so he would leave us alone, but most of the time he got around to us too.

I can remember how we used to all huddle together in the next room while he was beating her. We would just hold on to each other crying. Later Momma would come in and hold us too. She'd rock us and hold us. When I was thirteen I couldn't take it anymore. I was afraid that if I stayed, he would kill me. So I left. It was survival that motivated me at that point.

I remember standing outside on the corner, shivering and crying. I had nowhere to go, all I knew was that I couldn't go back home. While I was standing there a man came by and asked me what was wrong. I told him and he told me I could stay with him. I didn't know this man, but I figured he couldn't be any worse than what I left behind. The Lord was looking out for me, cause he wasn't crazy or anything. Later I married him.

After I moved out, my brothers and sisters would come and visit me. My place got to be sort of a hang out, a safe haven. My mother would come too, sometimes. Now that we are older, my brothers and sisters and I have talked. We decided that even though Momma was too weak to protect us, we always knew she loved us. She didn't want to see us beaten and hurt.

One by one all my brothers and sisters got out after I left. We are still real close. We check with each other all the time just to see if everything is okay. It's funny we all turned out just fine in spite of the way we grew up.

Sometimes a negative experience with a family member can be rechanneled into a positive experience.

Jane

I remember my ex-husband told me that I would never amount to anything. He said I'd never have a home, a car, you know, all of the things that are supposed to spell success. So, I just love the old "prove them wrong" theory. When people tell me you won't amount to anything, you won't do anything, or you won't have anything, I just work that much harder to be a success. I remember when I got my first car I drove past my ex-husband's house and blew the horn and waved! But, that's how I look at everything now. I don't let people put me down.

Black Women as Sisters

Black women have often relied upon friends who could be trusted to look after their children.

Ruth

When I was fifteen years old my mother and I fell out. I don't even re-member what it was all about now. But I was mad. So I decided that I'd get even and run away. I packed up my bag and went over to my god-mother's house. She was glad to see me. She told me to come right on in. We had a ball. I let her cook for me and she cooked all my favorite food. She even sent her husband out for the things they didn't have on hand (laughter).

I stayed there for a few days, then I started getting worried when nobody from home called for me or came by. What, didn't they miss me? What kind of parents did I have? I didn't know that she had called my mother almost as soon as I got there and told her I was safe, so don't worry. I went home, I think, that weekend. Mother acted like nothing happened. I don't think I ran away anymore after that.

Mae

I grew up listening to what I call "woman talk." My mother's friends would come by or she would talk to them on the phone. They would just laugh. My mother always seemed different when she was talking to her friends, younger and more relaxed.

Lou

I met my best friend when I was in third grade. She saved me from starving to death. This was during the depression and since there were so many of us, we fixed anything we could get our hands on for lunch, peanut butter and jelly was standard. Sometimes you just slam two pieces of bread together, this was a "jam sandwich" (laughter). But one girl's father kept his job during the depression and she and her sister had the best. She would come to school with nice ham sandwiches or tuna sandwiches. Things we couldn't afford and she would give them to me. She didn't want them. So we'd trade sandwiches. When she moved away, I really missed her.

But we moved a few years later and when I went to my new school and I walked into my room, there she was! I started to grin and so did she. She remembered me, too! We were always together after that. The thing I appreciated most about her was that she would listen. She wasn't much of a talker, you know, she'd say a few things. But I could trust that when I told her something, it wouldn't go any farther. A secret was safe with her.

Friends often are another source of encouragement and support.

Connie

Julie was like a person that made you feel good about yourself, even though you didn't feel so good at that time. I had come to the point where I sort of gave up on myself. I just folded. But with her and another friend, Donna, I could laugh and talk.

Tonia

I had the kind of family and the kind of friends that encouraged me because they believed in me. There were many times when I felt like I just wanted to throw my hands up. But I had strength behind me.

Annie

I had a friend that had a car. She'd come by and pick me up. Take me to school. She said, "Girl you are going to get this degree." So she took me each day. She'd watch my daughter for me when my mother couldn't. Yeah, I sure couldn't have gotten through without her.

Tia

Oddly enough it was a white woman who helped me out, who had the biggest influence in my life. She's the kind of woman I wish my mother had been. She can do things, she doesn't let things stand in her way. She'd say to me, "Now Tia, what is it that you want to do?" After I would tell her, she would sit down with me and work out a plan so it would happen.

Now that I'm in a career, I seek out other women who are like that. I'm meeting strong, Black women and I am encouraged by them. But my first influential person was a white woman.

Deep Spiritual Awareness

The Black religious experience has been important in uniting the Black community. It is common for African American women to have a strong church background.

Fannie

My mother always kept us in church and I loved going to church because that is where you get your spiritual guidance, your spiritual heading, but since I was sixteen I haven't been in church. ...[M]y kids don't go to church, sorry to say. They need to go to church, but I do have Bibles over the bed and we have Bible stories that they read.

Jane

I try to be an example. I go to church and Sunday school. I try to help people. I feel I am in a constant state of growing and becoming.

Tonia

I don't like going to church and staying three or four hours, but you gonna find me like you find the majority of the Black population in church on Sunday. Because that is our one source. The one thing we have in common is that we know what the Lord can do for us. I don't care how far you stray away, you always come back to the Lord.

Mrs. L (age 95)

I tell you where all my strength comes from. It comes from the Lord, plain and simple. Can't do nothing without the Lord. The fact that I'm still here today talking to you is through the grace of God.

Sometimes God is seen as having direct control over events.

Ellie

My husband had returned from military service and I don't know, he just couldn't handle it. He wasn't used to being part of the household and he wanted to know everything that was going on, everything that I was doing. And the kids and I weren't used to anyone asking. There was a lot of tension as he tried to exert this macho image. So it happened one day, he snapped. One night he just started shooting up the house. Of course I was trying to protect the children and I got shot, but in that moment I did not worry because I felt protected. I knew whatever he did I was going to be okay.

This woman discovered that God was not the reason for her painful past. This woman discovered that the human will can be very destructive.

Tia

Now that I'm grown, I've come to grips with God. I go to church. I realize that it wasn't because of God that I suffered so much as a child. God wasn't punishing me. It took a long time to realize that. I was abused because I had a father who had problems and a mother whose religion got in the way. It wasn't God, but a religious faith that was the problem.

Religion, for some, defined who they were as a person. This woman's community and family was the religious community she lived in.

Maggie

I was born in Louisiana, in a little village outside of New Orleans named St. Rose Parish. I had a Catholic upbringing.

Sister Joan

I early decided that I wanted to serve God, don't ask me where that came from, I would say the spirit, but now when I think about it I had gone to Catholic school and I liked the nuns, they were friendly, they related to me. I was a good student in school so they allowed me to get to know them more as people (of course now I know that they thought I was okay, an exception, you know). But as a child I felt I wanted to be a sister. But I didn't get much farther than that at the time. My remarks were met with more or less ambivalence. A black nun was unheard of.

It didn't come up again until I was about a senior in high school. I heard a sermon on the actual grace and awareness is the promise of the Holy Spirit. I was sitting there saying to myself, "How do you know that your desire to become a sister is not one of the promises of the Holy Spirit?" And running through my mind was, "If I don't try it in terms of sisterhood, will I regret that I should have or could have and ought to have later on in life?"

So off I went to the convent . . . [and] during those years of hardship I was still growing in grace with the Lord. In the prayers we said everyday, I certainly felt accepted by the Lord, affirmed by the Lord, and affirmed in terms that what I was doing was what the Lord wanted me to do. So even though all of this craziness was going on all around me at all levels, there was a communion going on; and I was hearing the Scriptures, hearing the Psalms. I would say that is the secret of my "success," my belief and my faith and my active relationship with the Lord.

Prayer is seen as the link between humans and God. It is the key to an active relationship with God.

Toni

It wasn't until maybe five or six years ago that I realized that I can be driving down the street and talk to Him like I'm talking to you and He would hear my prayer. I was like everyone else I guess, when I was younger I thought you had to get on your knees, and say "Lord, you gotta help me" and the Lord would hear your prayer. Then I realized that I didn't have to wait until something happened to talk to Him. I could just talk whenever I felt like it. I could say, "Lord, thank you for waking me up today." That was a prayer. And so I talked to a friend about it. And I said, "Teach me how to pray." And he said, "You've already got it. What do you think you're doing when you sing all of those songs?" He said, "I don't need to teach you how to pray." I thought about it and said,

"Well, I am praying." Sometimes it just takes somebody else to make you realize that you're already doing what you set out to do.

Black Community Connectedness

The African American woman has played a vital role in the Black community. With the church as a focus of activity, the Black woman has developed and sustained support networks. The spirit of cooperation is important in the Black community. It has been through struggle and sacrifice that African Americans have come from slavery and it is in that spirit that struggle for freedom continues today.

Jane

I have started taking troubled youth into my home. You know, they've fallen out with their parents or whatever. So instead of them going out on the streets, they come to my house. I wonder where this intrinsic need to help people comes from?

Maggie

Somewhere along the line I guess I began to wonder why it always seemed that the only thing I ever saw about Black people was derogatory. I thought, why is this when I knew better, I knew good things were going on. So I got interested in Black history and I took a class. It was the only class that really perked me up. For example . . . I'd be sitting in a regular history class, it was usually dull, the teacher would be talking about Christopher Columbus as they always did. But in Black history we'd talk about George Washington Carver and my mind would say, "Wake up!" I wanted to know more about these people and their contributions.

I realized later when I began teaching that the history books didn't include Black people because people didn't want you to know about them. If you didn't know what your people had done and had accomplished then you would never feel that you could do anything, you see.

So I think my main inspiration was finding out about the Black heroes and heroines. By reading about Mary McCleod-Bethune and how she started a college with five little girls in one little room with five orange crates for desks, then I thought maybe I can do that, too.

Sister Joan

I trace my success back to my parents, back to a family unit that came from the South. They grew up in the shadows of Tuskegee and had that kind of influence. They knew themselves as Black people in a racist society and yet they were nurtured because they were in a segregated Black community. Because of that, they were very learned about Black history and had Black values.

My parents had a thing about us developing ourselves to the best of our ability and developing our skill, being college educated – and all of that was for service to the community.

Tonia

When I was coming up, I lived in the kind of neighborhood where there was a lot of children; but if we came up to each other, one kid would say, "What you having for dinner tonight?" And if someone said, "Well, come over to my house to eat," then it was okay. Everyone fixed enough food to feed the whole neighborhood because you never knew if all the kids in the neighborhood was going to be at your house.

And then there is the satisfaction that comes from knowing that you have helped another person come along.

Fannie

I love my job. I love helping people, helping kids. I have over six hundred people, volunteers, on this side of town that depend on me. They say people in CHA are lazy; they don't want to do nothing. That's bull.

Jane

I'm also working with a younger Black female who has been discriminated against. I'm now trying to work with her and build her up. I'm also dealing with the people who discriminated against her. I mean I know from experience how it is with some white folks. They are not even aware sometimes of how they are. Racism is so deep, you know. So now I'm dealing with them in ways they are not used to.

Appendix B:
A Sample Interview

In each interview after introductions and a brief explanation of the study, each of the women were asked to give their life stories. These stories were told with very few interruptions from the researcher. All interruptions or questions were for clarity only. Generally, all of the interviews lasted between 45 minutes and an hour and a half. This is an interview in its entirety.

F.J.: Well, my name is Fannie Jones. I'm a fifteen-year resident of the Chicago Housing Authority. I am now the LAC president, which is the Local Advisory Council president of the development where I live. I'm also working for the Chicago Housing Authority in the Summer Food Service Program, which feeds twenty-two thousand children during the summer months. They eat lunch and seventeen thousand eat breakfast.

I think most Black women, well myself, I think I get all of my strengths and hidden powers from my mother. It started from a little girl up. My mother had thirteen children, and I have seen my mother give birth to two of my sisters and brothers one day and the next day she was back at her job. Back then, you know the only jobs Black folks did was working in the hospital or cleaning toilets or whatever. My mother worked in a hospital laundry, one that was filthy and dirty. She had to stand on her feet all day and fold sheets and what have you. And like I say, she would give birth on one day and the next day we would be thinking she was in bed and find out she had gone to work. Sometimes she had to work two jobs, there were thirteen of us and we had to eat. Just to buy shoes, food and rent, she had to work two jobs. My father was there. He was working also. He had one job. My mother had two jobs.

When my mother wasn't home, my father was there. And you know at that time birth control pills weren't as prevalent, at least not for Black women as it was for white women. Black folks just had babies back then. Until the economy realized that it wasn't that good for Black women to keep having babies. Now they're shoving birth control pills, and abortions, and whatever at us.

But I think it is important for Black women to know that we have come so far. Another thing that has made me strong is all of the trials and tribulations I have come through at my age. I'm thirty-five years old. I know that all the women that's my age or maybe two years older or two years younger, they had mothers like I had. They had the struggle to make ends meet. You saw it right there. The right type of mother really cares about her kids—that was instilled in all Black women. I feel that Black women are strong because they've got no choice.

You know the society, the way it is today, has pushed the Black male out of the house. And with it a lot of people are on public aid or some type of assistance, not by choice but by force. Such as my mother, she really didn't have no choice. When she was coming up, she couldn't go to school. Schools weren't really that open to Black women at that time. My mother had only two sisters and a brother; they also had to work hard to keep food on the table. And so, therefore, by your mother having to work days and then having to come home to a house full of kids, that meant that all of us had to work. Some of us did have very good jobs. I'd say half of us had good jobs, the other half did not. Coming from such a large family, there is always going to be somebody that doesn't do so good.

E.P.: So do you think most Black women are strong because of their children?

F.J.: If you're a mother and you really love your children, then, you know, those children did not ask to come here and they don't know nothing. You owe them. If you really love your child, then it's up to you to provide for that child and for that child's future and you have to be strong, you have to look out for the child. In my household, I know my mother used to always say, "My kids are number one, my kids come first." My mother would go without eating just to make sure that all of us had food and she would be the last one to eat. And sometimes she would just eat the leftovers from the plates. I know what my mother was saying, but I say, I'm number one. Because I say, if I'm not, well, if I'm not together, then I can't help you. So I've got to be able to help myself in order to help you. You have to be able to help youself before you can help someone else. If you're always looking out for everyone else without looking out for yourself first, then you have a lot of shortcomings, a lot of headaches, a lot of frustrations and disappointments. The things that I do to help others is helping me out too . . . so I'm still helping myself.

So, number one, I love me and it goes back to my mother and father. I really admire my mother. I mean, to see her have babies and go right back to work, walk through snow when the buses wouldn't run. I have seen her walk seven or eight miles to work and she'd say, "It doesn't matter, I've got to feed my kids." My mother would always say, "You think highly of yourself. Make yourself number one, whether no one in this world loves you or not, you've got to love you. If you don't the world can hurt you. If you love youself, can't nobody take that from you. All that you get, you going to have to go out there and earn." That's why I think so highly of myself. I loves me and I loves living and I loves helping people. Every time people comes to me that I can help – every ten people, if I can help two or three, that makes me feel happy.

I'm still real close to my family. I mean my other sisters and brothers. We are very, very close. We fuss and fight like normal sisters and brothers. We get on each other's nerves, but we don't let nobody else do it. We love each other, we gets along. And that's hard to believe for some people, that there are thirteen of us and we all really gets along. I have a brother that's in California, one in Denver, a sister that's in Colorado, too, but we keep in touch. I think that's because of my mother too. My mother always was telling me that no matter how much I fuss and fight and get on other people's nerves, remember that she was my mother. She said, "No matter what happens, ya'll will have to come back and see me [laughter]. So long as ya'll are living, ya'll are going to bump heads. But when I'm gone, all you'll have is each other."

She had very high standards for all of us, too. Yes, she did. She was from the old school, she was from down South. Her grandmother raised her until she passed away. So she would buy our clothes from little stores or different Catholic churches. We never had brand new clothes, but that didn't make no difference. My mother would go to these stores and buy big boxes of these used clothes, she would wash them, starch and iron them. She used to keep our hair combed, keep us nice and clean. She used to always win the award at the school for the best-dressed and cleanest kids. People used to ask her how she did it.

And I feel that even though the situation is changing and the economy is changing, anything can be taught, and I can learn it. There's no such thing as I can't learn and I can't do. Sometimes people's pride gets in the way. There's illiterate women out there, but they can comprehend, they can do a job. Like sometimes people will ask, "Mrs. Jones, can you do this?" No, I hadn't done it before, but I wasn't going to tell them I couldn't do it. Then I wouldn't get a chance. So I tell them, "Yeah, I can do it. Just give me a chance." I did not know anything about it, but now

I'm running half of CHA. I have over seven hundred people, volunteers up under me. They come in every Friday to see me. The development that I'm at has over ten thousand people at it and I'm over that. If they have a banged-up ceiling, they come to me. If their toilet's leaking, they come to me. They come if they want to know how to get into a program or how to get grants for their kids to go to college. They call me at home (I try not to give out my home number); and when I get home from work, people are sitting on my porch lined up (laughter). Those that I can help, I help. Those I cannot, I try to refer to somebody who can. I know one thing, when the Lord comes, they'll say, "Well, if Mrs. Jones couldn't help me, she sure sent me to somebody who could even if she had to call all the way to Springfield to find them."

It's all in being self-confident and knowing the right people. I enjoy going to different meetings. I enjoy going to workshops because I get to meet people and find out what they can and cannot do. Therefore, I use them as a resource guide, resources so people can go to them if I know someone is in a particular situation or predicament.

E.P.: Do you have any other plans or goals that you can use your resources and connections for?

F.J.: I do have some political aspirations. I'm planning to run for alderman and I feel I could win, hands down. I'm not sure though, I think sometimes I'm not devious enough, or hypocritical enough to make a good politician. I believe in being fair and I believe in telling the truth. It sometimes hurt more if I tell the truth on a person, than to tell lies. So if I go into the political arena, they are going to have to watch out. Harold Washington ain't going to be nothing compared to Fannie Jones. I've had other job offers in CHA as well. I've had the offers, which I should have taken, it's not like I don't need the money. But I figured that if I'm going to do something, it's going to be something that I want to do, something that I enjoy doing, not something that somebody else wants me to do. My father always said, "Whatever you do make sure that it's something that you want, something that you're satisfied with, because if not, you'd either be fighting or you'd become disappointed and frustrated."

Even if it's a lower paying job and it's something I enjoy doing and I'm helping people, then I don't mind. Pay is nothing to helping someone else. I always say, I always feel great when I know I have stooped down and helped someone else stand. There's no greater feeling, no greater joy. It's too many people out there that needs help, for someone to go around being selfish, being self-centered. I look no better than no one else. I'm just like the next person. What I have I got because other people have helped me. I never look down on people, I never turn my nose up. If I have it then thank God, if they have it then I'm happy for them.

E.P.: Are you involved with tenant management, then?

F.J.: No, I'm not. Tenant management is fine and great and they give you money to do the interior, but it's the exterior that I'm worried about. It's okay to give me money to fix up my building, to fix up my development, but these same buildings have been standing for 35 years. We have pipe corrosion on the inside, we had to start from the bottom up, work our way from the inside out, not from the outside in. And it would take millions of dollars in order to get it the way it should be. Tenant management is nice and all for tenant managers.

If I were in tenant management, I would like to declare martial law. It's just the neighborhood of the people that live there. You know I would live in CHA forever, I would not leave, I love my building... All the CHA developments are on prime locations. You have transportation north, south, east, and west. If CHA would uphold their rules, it could be another Garden of Eden. It really could be a paradise. You know that most of our households, it's about a hundred and seventy thousand authorized people living in CHA and out of that a hundred and sixty thousand of them are women as head of household. Mr. Lang is recognizing that we have great respect for the women that's the head of these households. He is bringing a lot of the political programs and a lot of resident employment and resident empowerment workshops, training and what have you. He recognizes that without the Black woman, this community cannot make it. Because they always say that behind every successful man is a strong woman, I say behind every successful man is a strong Black woman.

Like I say, most of the people in CHA are women. The problem is now the teenagers have taken over. The Black women out there need some help. These young ones need to be guided in the right directions. All of them are not sitting home everyday, some of them are going to school, some of them are going to work. Some of them have been locked out, though. They've been told, "No, you can't when all they needed was someone to tell them "Yes, you can." Sometimes you have to spoonfeed them, what I mean is walk them through the door and help them fill out a form or go sit with them two or three times or track with them until they know their way around. Once you walk them through that door, if they are sincere, then they are going to follow through. Number one, if I have them, do something, they don't want to disappoint me ... because I've put so much time, and so much faith in them. I don't want to save the world. Just a little part of it. My husband helps me out, too. When I'm not home, people have started going to him.

E.P.: You made a comment a few minutes ago about the teenagers taking over. What about this?

F.J.: There is nothing constructive for our teenagers to do today. In my development, we have more girl gangs than we do boy gangs; and I was a tomboy and used to climb fences, but I never carried knives, sticks, bottles, bats, and guns. I never did any of that, and I was a tomboy during childhood. There's nothing constructive for them to do. First, they are priced out of the job market. And even so, in Wendy's or McDonald's, it just ain't worth it. They gotta take abuse all day long and you work under unsafe conditions. . . The young lady not too long ago got a third degree burn. They turn out abusive and disrespectful because grownups are abusive and disrespectful to them.

Or they decide to imitate the drug pushers. Peer pressure can do it; they want the clothes and the cars, you know, make the money. And in just a few more years, they'll be locked up or they'll be dead because somebody gonna kill them. But some of them use that money to support their families. I've seen them. I know one boy, he dropped out of school, started selling drugs. He filled the house with furniture, all of the kids got decent beds, he sent all of his brothers and sisters to school. I told him, "That ain't the right way to get it, stay in school." But he's hollering, "I'm 17 now. Look how long I'd have to wait to get a job."

But I don't know, we have to do something and the Black women are just going to have to stick together. They are going to have to pull themselves up. Just like I say, if you can be taught, you can learn it. Ain't nobody gonna give you nothing; ain't nobody gonna hand you nothing. You may not get everything that you pay for, but you are going to pay for everything you get. That's my philosophy. So you've got to believe in yourself. You've got to have that self-love. If you love yourself, then you can love anyone. If you're miserable, then you are going to make everybody around you miserable. You always think the best of you. I always. . . I can be mad at the world when I come to work, but nobody knows it because I try to leave it at home. And when I go back home, hey, I'm not mad at anybody anymore. It's funny. . . It's just a temporary inconvenience. You know, it doesn't pay to go to bed mad. Go to bed with a smile because Satan is busy. Satan is everywhere.

When I was younger, up to age fourteen, we live next door to a church. We attended every day. When we moved, we moved next door to a church! My mother always kept us in church and I loved going to church because that is where you get your spiritual guidance, your spiritual healing, but since I was sixteen I haven't been in church. I haven't been in church in years and my kids don't go to church, sorry to say. They need to go to church, but I do have Bibles over the bed and we have Bible stories that they read. They know the difference between right and wrong and being selfish and looking out for others.

I tell them to look out for each other. You know, what you learn as a child, then you turn it back. I haven't had any problems so far; they haven't caused me any grief or heartaches. When comes to education, I don't even have to deal with that. My husband stays on them about that. He tells them that education is the only way out. My one son has perfect attendance. And my other son got all of the awards at his school except perfect attendance (he had a sore throat).

Look, you get out of your child what you put into your child. Your child has got to have that positive image, that positive mental attitude and he gets it from his parents, mother, father or both of them. I go to different meetings, I go to different events and I take my children with me. That way they can see that I am involved. You can only want as far as you can see. If all my children ever know is a CHA housing development, that's all they will ever know. The more you see, the more you experience, the more you want, the more you have an idea of what you might want to become, and what you might not want to become.

Well, finally I'll say, I love my job. I love helping people, helping kids. I have over six hundred people, volunteers, on this side of town that depend on me. They say people in CHA are lazy; they don't want to do nothing. That's bull. We got people... The trucks are here at five forty-five in the morning. We got people here at four forty-five waiting to receive in the meals. They are feeding all of these hundred to hundred and fifty kids. The kids make a mess, and they stay to clean up the site. They bring they own wash powder, they own bleach. That's giving these ladies something to do. I mean, it's giving them a reason to get up, to comb their hair, to put on some clothes, and look decent. It's getting them to apply themselves. It gives people something to do.

I love helping people feel better about themselves. Two of the women came back to me and told me they had done what I told them to do and it worked. They wanted to thank me. I told them, "Don't thank me, just continue what you doing and make me proud. That's thanks enough. You don't have to give me nothing, just make me proud of you, be proud of yourself, make your kids proud of you."

Well, I've got a meeting tonight with the area director, and I know it's going to be positive. I don't mind going straight to the top. I've ain't got nothing to lose. And one thing about it, I love telling the truth. So as long as I tell the truth, I ain't got nothing to worry about.

Notes

Introduction

1. Brian Lanker, *I Dream a World* (New York: Stewart, Tabori, Chang, 1989), p. 8.

2. Langston Hughes, "Mother to Son," in *Selected Poems Langston Hughes* (New York: Vintage Books, 1959), p. 187.

Chapter 1

3. St. Augustine, *The Confessions of St. Augustine,* 10th book (Westwood, NJ: Christian Library, 1984), p. 165.

4. Silvano Arieti, *The Will to Be Human* (New York: Quadrangle Books, 1972), p. 10.

5. Joseph Rychlak, *Discovering Free Will and Personal Responsibility* (New York: Oxford University Press, 1979), p. 11.

6. Ibid, pp. 12–15.

7. Sherman Stanage, *Adult Education and Phenomenological Research* (Malabar, FL: Krieger Pub. Co., 1987), pp. 38–39.

8. R. G. Collingwood, *An Essay on Metaphysics* (Lanham, MD: University Press of America, 1972), pp. 290–293.

9. Ibid., p. 296.

10. Ibid., p. 324.

11. Ibid., p. 325.

12. Rychlak, *Discovering Free Will,* p. 10.

13. Arieti, *The Will to Be Human,* p. 47.

14. Ibid., p. 48.

15. Maxine Greene, *The Dialectic of Freedom* (New York: Teachers College Press, 1988), p. 90.

16. Ibid., pp. 88–89.

17. Rychlak, *Discovering Free Will,* p. 17.

18. St. Anselm, *Basic Writings,* "The Monologiu," chapters 10 and 11, trans. S. N. Deane (Lasalle, IL: Open Court Pub. Co., 1962), pp. 57–58.

19. Gen. 1:27–28. [All passages are taken from the *Good News Bible*.]

20. Gen. 3:4.

21. Gen. 22:12.

22. Rychlak, *Discovering Free Will*, p. 71; also see discussion of St. Augustine in Bernard Haring, *General Moral Theology*, vol. 1: *Free and Faithful in Christ* (New York: Seabury Press, 1974), pp. 40–42.

23. St. Augustine, *The Confessions of St. Augustine*, p. 101.

24. Rychkak, *Discovering Free Will*, p. 72.

25. Erasmus and Luther, *Discourse on Free Will*, ed. Ernst F. Winter (New York: Frederick Unger, 1974).

26. Haring, *General Moral Theology*, pp. 113–114.

27. Hans Kung, *Does God Exist: An Answer for Today*, trans. Edward Quinn (Garden City, NY: Doubleday, 1980), p. 674.

28. Ibid., p. 428.

29. Ibid., p. 495.

30. Ibid., p. 18.

31. Rollo May, *Love and Will* (New York: W. W. Norton, 1969), p. 220.

32. William James, *Principles of Psychology*, vol. 2 (Toronto: Henry Holt, 1890; reprint ed., New York: Dover Publishing, 1950).

33. William James, "What the Will Effects," in *Essays in Psychology*, ed. Frederick Burkhardt (Cambridge, MA: Harvard University Press, 1983), p. 231.

34. Friedrich Nietzsche, *The Will to Power*, trans. Walter Kaufmann and R. J. Hollingdale, ed. Walter Kaufmann (New York: Vintage Books, 1968), p. 84.

35. Kung, *Does God Exist*, p. 358.

36. Arthur Schopenhauer, *The World as Will and Idea*, quoted in Kung, *Does God Exist*, p. 359.

37. Ibid., p. 361.

38. Nietzsche, *The Will to Power*, p. 79.

39. Ibid., p. 29.

40. Ibid., p. 129.

41. John Watson, quoted in Rychlak, *Discovering Free Will*, pp. 38–39.

42. B. F. Skinner, quoted in Arieti, *The Will to Be Human*, p. 7.

43. Rychlak, *Discovering Free Will*, p. 38.

44. May, *Love and Will*, p. 207.

45. Robert Assagioli, *The Act of Will* (New York: Penguin Books, 1973), p. 9.

46. Ibid., pp. 7–8.

47. Arieti, *The Will to Be Human*, p. 15.

48. Assagioli, *The Act of Will*, p. 10.

49. Ibid., p. 89.

50. Ibid., p. 110.

51. Ibid., p. 135.

52. Ibid., p. 138.

53. Jeremiah Wright, sermon, *Evolution vs. Creation,* Trinity United Church of Christ, Chicago, 9 March 1988.

54. Joseph White, *The Psychology of Blacks: An Afro-American Perspective* (Englewood Cliffs, NJ: Prentice-Hall, 1984), p. 33.

55. Katie Cannon, *Black Womanist Ethics* (Atlanta Scholars Press, 1988).

Chapter 2

56. Herbert Spiegelberg, quoted in Sherman Stanage, *Adult Education and Phenomenological Research,* (Malabor, FL: Krieger Pub. Co., 1987), p. 43.

57. Martin Heidegger, *Being and Time,* trans. John Macquarrie and Edward Robinson (Tubingen, Germany: Neomarius Verlag; reprint ed. New York: Harper and Row, 1962), p. 58.

58. Stanage, *Adult Education,* p. 93.

59. James Edie, *Edmund Husserl's Phenomenology* (Bloomington: Indiana University Press, 1987), p. 2.

60. Ibid., p. 3.

61. Heidegger, *Being and Time,* p. 59.

62. Ibid., p. 4.

63. Alfred Schutz, *The Phenomenology of the Social World,* trans. George Walsh and Frederick Lehnert (Chicago: Northwestern University Press, 1967), pp. 36–37.

64. Edmund Husserl, quoted in Schutz, *Phenomenology of the Social World,* p. 36.

65. For the seven steps of the phenomenological approach, see Herbert Speigelberg, *The Phenomenological Movement,* 3rd ed. (The Hague: Martinus Nijhoff, 1982), pp. 682–715.

66. Stanage, *Adult Education,* p. 26.

67. Duncan S. Ferguson, *Biblical Hermeneutics, An Introduction* (Atlanta: John Knox Press, 1986), p. 4.

68. Ibid., p. 5.

69. William Outhwaithe, "Hans-Georg Gadamer," in *The Return of Grand Theory in the Human Sciences,* ed. Quentin Skinner (Cambridge, England: Cambridge University Press, 1985), p. 25.

70. Hans-Georg Gadamer, *Truth and Method* (New York: Seabury Press, 1975), pp. 273–274.

71. Kelly Miller Smith, *Social Crisis Preaching* (Macon, GA: Mercer University Press, 1984).

72. Henry H. Mitchell, *Black Preaching* (San Francisco: Harper and Row, 1970, 1979), p. 30.

73. Ibid., p. 28.

74. Howard Thurman, *The Creative Encounter* (Richmond, IN: Friends United Press, 1972), p. 31.

75. Howard Thurman, "Growing into Life," in *For the Inward Journey* (New York: Harcourt Brace Jovanovich, 1981), p. 20.

Chapter 3

76. Mary Helen Washington, ed., Introduction to *Midnight Birds* (Garden City, NY: Anchor Books, 1980), p. xiii.

77. Katie Cannon, *Black Womanist Ethics* (Atlanta: Scholars Press, 1988), p. 87.

78. Alice Walker, quoted in Robert E. Hemenway, *Zora Neale Hurston: A Literary Biography* (Urbana: University of Illinois Press, 1977), p. xii.

79. Cannon, p. 125.

80. Ibid.

81. Ibid.

82. Zora Neale Hurston, "The Gilded Six Bits," in *I Love When I Am Laughing and Then Again When I Am Looking Mean and Impressive*, ed. Alice Walker (New York: Feminist Press, 1979), pp. 208–218.

83. Ibid., p. 210.

84. Ibid., p. 211.

85. Ibid., p. 216.

86. Zora Neale Hurston, *Jonah's Gourd Vine* (Philadelphia: J. B. Lippincott, 1934; reprint ed., New York: Harper and Row, 1990), p. 3.

87. Ibid., p. 5.

88. Ibid., p. 79.

89. Ibid., p. 88.

90. Ibid., p. 98.

91. Ibid., pp. 121–122.

92. Ibid., p. 131.

93. Ibid., p. 130.

94. Hemenway, *Zora Neale Hurston*, p. 231.

95. Zora Neale Hurston, *Their Eyes Were Watching God* (Philadelphia: J. B. Lippincott, 1937), p. 9.

96. Ibid., pp. 31, 37.

97. Ibid., p. 44.

98. Ibid., p. 119.

99. Bessie W. Jones and Audrey Vinson, *The World of Toni Morrison: Explorations in Literary Criticism* (Dubuque, IA: Kendall Hunt Pub. Co., 1985), p. 7.

100. Ibid., p. 50.

101. Ibid.

102. Toni Morrison, interviewed by Bessie W. Jones and Audrey Vinson, *The World of Toni Morrison*, p. 142.

103. Ibid., p. 130.

104. Toni Morrison, *Sula* (New York: New American Library, 1973), p. 174.

105. Ibid., pp. 5, 6.

106. Ibid., p. 29.

107. Ibid., p. 52.

108. Ibid., p. 57.

109. Ibid., p. 95.

110. Ibid., p. 119.

111. Ibid., p. 145.

112. Ibid., p. 35.

113. Ibid., p. 36.

114. Ibid., p. 76.

115. Hortense Spellers, "The Politics of Intimacy: A Discussion," in *Sturdy Black Bridges*, ed. Bell, Parker, and Guy-Sheftall (Garden City, NJ: Anchor Books, 1979), p. 105.

116. Mary Helen Washington, "An Essay on Alice Walker," in *Sturdy Black Bridges*, ed. Bell, Parker, and Guy-Sheftall, p. 133.

117. Ibid., p. 137.

118. Alice Walker, *The Color Purple* (New York: Pocket Books, 1982).

119. The theme of the "suspended" woman is a recurrent theme in the works of Alice Walker. See *In Search of Our Mother's Gardens* (San Diego: Harcourt Brace Jovanovich, 1984); also "An Essay on Alice Walker," Mary Helen Washington, in *Sturdy Black Bridges*, ed. Bell, Parker, and Guy-Sheftall, pp. 133–149.

120. Mary Helen Washington, "An Essay on Alice Walker," in *Sturdy Black Bridges*, ed. Bell, Parker, and Guy-Sheftall, p. 138.

121. Walker, *The Color Purple*, p. 41.

122. Ibid., p. 44.

123. Alice Walker, *The Third Life of Grange Copeland* (New York: Harcourt Brace Jovanovich, 1970).

124. Ibid.

125. An interview with Alice Walker in *Sturdy Black Bridges*, ed. Bell, Parker, and Guy-Sheftall, p. 146.

126. Zora Neale Hurston, "How It Feels to Be Colored Me," in *I Love Myself When I Am Laughing*, pp. 152–155.

127. Hemenway, *Zora Neale Hurston*, p. 13.

128. Zora Neale Hurston, *Dust Tracks on a Road*, 2nd ed., ed. Robert E. Hemingway (Urbana: University of Illinois Press, 1942), pp. 58–59.

129. Bruce Nugent, quoted in Hemenway, *Zora Neale Hurston*, p. 70.

130. Hurston, *Dust Tracks on a Road*, pp. 58–59.

131. Ibid., p. 124.

132. Hemenway, *Zora Neale Hurston*, pp. 146–147.

133. Ibid., p. 321.

134. Alice Walker, "Looking for Zora," in *I Love Myself When I Am Laughing*, p. 307.

135. Mary Burgher, "Images of Self and Race in the Autobiographies of Black Women," in *Sturdy Black Bridges*, ed. Bell, Parker, and Guy-Sheftall, pp. 107–121.

136. Ibid., p. 113.

137. Maya Angelou, *I Know Why the Caged Bird Sings* (New York: Random House, 1969), p. 2.

138. Mary Burgher, "Images of Self and Race," p. 116.

139. Maya Angelou, *Gather Together in My Name* (New York: Random House, 1974), p. 24.

140. Ibid., pp. 27, 28.

Chapter 4

141. Murray, Pauli, "Jim Crow and Jane Crow," taken from *Black Women in White America*, ed. Gerda Lerner (New York: Vintage, 1972).

142. Paula Giddings, *When and Where I Enter: The Impact of Black Women on Race and Sex in America* (New York: William Morrow, 1984), p. 43.

143. Daniel P. Moynihan, *The Negro Family: The Case for National Action* (Washington, DC: U.S. Dept. of Labor, 1965).

144. Vivian Gordon, *Black Woman, Feminism and Black Liberation: Which Way* (Chicago: Third World Press, 1987), p. viii.

145. Angela Y. Davis, *Women, Culture, and Politics* (New York: Random House, 1989), p. 74.

146. Maxine Greene, *The Dialectic of Freedom* (New York: Teachers College Press, 1988), p. 66.

147. Gordon, *Black Women*, p. 19.

148. Joseph White, *The Psychology of Blacks: An Afro-American Perspective* (Englewood Cliffs, NJ: Prentice-Hall, 1984), p. 35.

149. Ibid., p. 88.

150. Ibid., pp. 62–63.

151. James H. Cone, *My Soul Looks Back* (Nashville: Abingdon, 1982), p. 20.

152. Gordon, *Black Women*, p. 24.

153. John Mbiti, quoted in Cecil Wayne Cone, *The Identity Crisis in Black Theology* (Nashville: AMEC, Henry Belin, Pub., 1975), p. 34.

154. Cecil Cone, *The Identity Crisis*, p. 35.

155. C. Eric Lincoln, *Race, Religion and the Continuing American Dilemma* (New York: Hill and Wang, 1984), p. 137.

156. James Cone, *My Soul Looks Back*, pp. 63, 137.

157. Ibid., pp. 22–23.

158. Ibid., p. 47.

159. White, *The Psychology of Blacks*, p. 3.

160. Ibid., p. 5.

Chapter 5

161. The Rev. Francis Grimke, quoted in *We Are Your Sisters/Black Women in the Nineteenth Century*, ed. Dorothy Sterling (New York: W. W. Norton, 1984), p. 403.

162. Joseph White, *The Psychology of Blacks: An Afro-American Perspective* (Englewood Cliffs, NJ: Prentice-Hall, 1984), p. 3.

163. Maxine Greene, *The Dialectic of Freedom* (New York: Teachers College Press, 1988), p. 95.

164. From the speech "I Have a Dream," delivered at the march on Washington, August 28, 1963, Lincoln Memorial, Washington, D.C.

165. Carter G. Woodson, *The Mis-Education of the Negro* (Washington, DC: Associated Publishers, 1933; reprint ed., Trenton, NJ: African World Press, 1990), p. 22.

166. Ibid.

167. C. Eric Lincoln, *Race, Religion and the Continuing American Dilemma* (New York: Hill and Wang, 1984), p. 198.

Annotated Bibliography

Angelou, Maya. *All God's Children Need Traveling Shoes*. New York: Vintage Books, 1986.
    Autobiography: Angelou writes about her experiences living in West Africa while her teenaged son recovers from a near fatal accident.

_____. *Gather Together in My Name*. New York: Bantam Books, 1974.
    Autobiography: Recounts Maya Angelou's life as a young woman and single parent in the late 1940s. Angelou talks candidly about her struggles and triumphs.

_____. *The Heart of a Woman*. New York: Bantam Books, 1984.
    Autobiography: Maya Angelou, now a singer-dancer, moves into the fast paced life of New York City. She joins the Harlem Writer's Guild and discovers she has a talent for writing. Maya becomes increasingly involved in the Civil Rights Movement and becomes the Northern coordinator working for Dr. Martin Luther King. After marrying an African freedom fighter, Angelou moves to Cairo and continues her inner struggle to find love and true commitment.

_____. *I Know Why the Caged Bird Sings*. New York: Bantam Books, 1969.
    Autobiography: The first of Maya Angelou's series. The book begins with the three year old Maya traveling to Stamps, Arkansas, to be raised by her paternal grandmother. Here under the strict tutelage of her grandmother, Maya learned about struggle, hard work, dignity, truth, and love.

_____. *Singin, Swingin, and Getting Merry Like Christmas*. New York: Bantam Books, 1976.
    Autobiography: Maya Angelou writes about the beginning of her career in show business. She reveals her failed attempt at an interracial marriage and her struggles as a young mother.

Arieti, Silvano. *The Will to Be Human*. New York: Quadrangle Books, 1972.
    Philosophy: Discusses our unique ability as humans to act within a limited will. Human will is limited by physical, environmental, social, and emotional conditions, yet as humans we alone share with God the power to create.

Asante, Molefi. *Afrocentricity*. Trenton, NJ: Africa World Press, 1988.

African American studies: Asante presents the theory that African American culture is based on an African world view that is contrary to the world view of Western cultures.

Assagioli, Robert. *The Act of Will*. New York: Penguin Books, 1973.

Sociology: The author outlines four dimensons of the human will: the strong will, the skillful will, the good will, and the transpersonal will. Also discussed are the stages of will development.

Burgher, Mary. "Images of Self and Race in the Autobiographies of Black Women." In *Sturdy Black Bridges*, edited by Roseann Bell, Bettye Parker, and Beverly Guy-Sheftall, pp. 107–121. Garden City, NJ: Anchor Books, 1979.

Essay: The author writes about autobiography as a valid source of information about the Black woman. She recognizes the autobiographies of Black women as a critical inquiry into the lives of the women writing them and as an attempt on their part to lay to rest the myths and labels that have surrounded them.

Cannon, Katie. *Black Womanist Ethics*. Atlanta: Scholars Press, 1988.

Christian ethics, African American studies: This study discusses the distinctive moral character of African American women. This moral character can be witnessed in the invisible dignity, quiet grace, and unshouted courage exhibited by many African American women. It begins with a history of the African American woman's situation in America, and then traces the development of the Black woman's literary tradition.

Carby, Hazel. *Reconstructing Womanhood: The Emergence of the Afro-American Woman Novelist*. New York: Oxford University Press, 1987.

History, Criticism: A critical analysis of the writings of Harriet Jacobs, Frances Ellen Harper, Anna Julia Cooper, Nella Larsen and other Black female writers. She examines the cultural position of the Black woman intellectual and explores the ways in which Black female writers have represented the prevailing ideological debates of their times.

Collingwood, R. G. *An Essay on Metaphysics*. Lanham, MD: University Press of America, 1972.

Philosophy: Collingwood revisits Aristotle's debate on causation and outlines three senses of causation. Collingwood comes to the conclusion that belief in causation is based on a conception that God is a semi-anthropomorphic being, meaning that God created man out of His supreme will and in so doing created a being that could will.

Cone, Cecil Wayne. *The Identity Crisis in Black Theology*. Nashville: AMEC, Henry Belin, Pub., 1975.

Theology: Discusses the relationship between traditional African religious thought, which was non–Christian, and present day African American religious tradition. Cone examines the basic tenets of African traditional religion and the basic tenets of Christianity and finds them comparable. The understanding of religion that the African people brought with them to America was the beginning of the strength of the church in the Black community.

Cone, James. *My Soul Looks Back*. Nashville: Abingdon, 1982.
    Theology: James Cone reflects on a relationship between God and Black people that is active and not passive. He discusses the role of the Black church in fostering the belief that Black people must work with God and that the Kingdom will only come with people and God working together.

Davis, Angela Y. *Women, Culture, and Politics*. New York: Random House, 1989.
    African American studies: In a book of essays, lectures, speeches, and other writings, the author addresses the struggle of women to achieve racial, sexual, and eonomic equality. Central themes include fair and adequate education, housing, health and child care. She critiques recent policy decisions and frames the debates in a much broader social context.

Donagan, Alan. *The Later Philosophy of R. G. Collingwood*. Chicago: University of Chicago Press, 1985.
    Philosophy: An analysis of R. G. Collingwood's major philosophical works. The author begins with an analysis of Collingwood's philosophy of mind. He then examines the distinction Collingwood made between feeling and perception, his theory of concepts and propositions, and his analysis of practical and theoretical thinking. The author concludes the first part of his book by investigating Collingwood's analysis of imagination, emotion, and expression, and his application of them to the philosophy of art. Understanding the relationship between feeling a phenomenon, experiencing the phenomenon, and then understanding the phenomenon is essential in phenomenological inquiry.

Edie, James. *Edmund Husserl's Phenomenology*. Bloomington: Indiana University Press, 1987.
    Philosophy: A discussion of phenomenology as a research method and an explanation of why it has been a popular method for students and readers of philosophy.

Ferguson, Duncan S. *Biblical Hermeneutics: An Introduction*. Atlanta: John Knox Press, 1986.
    Theology: An overview of Biblical hermeneutics: its history, method, and implementation. This is a helpful text for those interested in Biblical interpretation.

Gadamer, Hans-Georg. *Truth and Method*. New York: Seabury Press, 1975.
    Social philosophy: An exploration into meaning and how people come to know and understand a text. A refined approach to hermeneutical interpretation.

Giddings, Paula. *When and Where I Enter: The Impact of Black Women on Race and Sex in America.* New York: William Morrow, 1984.

African American studies: Addresses the struggle of Black women to maintain dignity in a society that viewed them as chattel. The author also touches upon the relationship between the Black mother and her children, especially the daughters, in that the mother understood that it was her responsibility to pass on the values and coping strategies that would enable them to survive in a racist society.

Gordon, Vivian. *Black Women, Feminism and Black Liberation: Which Way?* Chicago: Third World Press, 1987.

African American studies: This book explores questions concerning Black women and feminism such as: Is it strictly a white woman's movement? What do Black women have to gain by involving themselves in feminist causes? The historical relationship between women's issues and the Black liberation movement is addressed in detail.

Greene, Maxine. *The Dialectic of Freedom.* New York: Teachers College Press, 1988.

Education philosophy: A thorough examination of the relationship between the social and moral struggle, and freedom. The author offers a definition of freedom. The book concludes with a charge to educators to create in their classrooms a place where students can act out their freedom.

Haring, Bernard. *General Morale Theology.* Vol. 1: *Free and Faithful in Christ.* New York: Seabury Press, 1974.

Theology: Offers an analysis of free will from the perspective of the early Roman Catholic church and from a more contempory view.

Heidegger, Martin. *Being and Time.* Translated by John Macquarrie and Edward Robinson. Tubingen, Germany: Neomarius Verlag, 1927; reprint ed. New York: Harper and Row, 1962.

Philosophy: Defines the phenomenological approach to inquiry. According to Heidegger all inquiry begins as a quest to get to "the things themselves" or to the heart of the phenomenon.

_____. *The Question of Being.* Translated by William Kluback and Jean T. Wilde. New Haven: College and University Press, 1958.

Philosophy: In a letter to Ernst Junger, Heidegger reinterprets Nietzsche. Heidegger uses the analogy of a line as a means of understanding nihilism.

Hemenway, Robert E. *Zora Neale Hurston.* Urbana: The University of Illinois Press, 1977.

Biography: A highly readable account of the life and work of Zora Neale Hurston, a model of Black individualism and achievement. The book is also a valuable sourcebook for those interested in the Harlem Renaissance period.

Hughes, Langston. "Mother to Son." In *Selected Poems Langston Hughes*, p. 187. New York: Vintage Books 1959.

Poetry: Mother relates to son the struggle of Black people. By telling him that life "ain't been no crystal stair" she prepares him for the challenges he must face as a Black man. This kind of preparation is often seen as a responsibility by Black women.

Hurston, Zora Neale. *Dust Tracks on a Road*, 2nd ed. Edited by Robert E. Hemenway. Urbana: University of Illinois Press, 1942.

Autobiography: Zora Neale Hurston's personal account of her life. A central theme are the "visions" that began when she was about eight years old. This theme suggest that Hurston was guided by a "destiny" or fate which was beyond her control.

_____. "How It Feels to Be Colored Me." In *I Love Myself When I'm Laughing and Then Again When I Am Looking Mean and Impressive*, edited by Alice Walker, pp. 152–155. New York: Feminist Press, 1979.

Essay: A very controversial response to those who in the time of the Harlem Renaissance depicted Black people as a tragic and victimized race. Hurston writes about the positive side of the Black experience. She expresses herself with a very characteristic pride and individualism.

_____. *Jonah's Gourd Vine*. Philadelphia: J. B. Lippincott, 1934; reprint ed., New York: Harper and Row, 1990.

Fiction: Zora Neale Hurston's first novel. The central character of this novel is John Pearson, but it is his wife Lucy who emerges as a true heroine. Lucy is a woman of great strength and wisdom. While she is alive she protects and supports her wayward husband, John.

_____. *Their Eyes Were Watching God*. Philadelphia: J. B. Lippincott, 1937.

Fiction: Considered Hurston's masterpiece. The love story of Janie Crawford, a young woman who through struggle comes to accept and understand life in a new way. In this novel Hurston draws greatly from the Black folk traditions of the rural South.

James, William. *Principals of Psychology*. Vol. 2. Toronto: Henry Holt, 1890; reprint ed., New York: Dover Publishers, 1950.

Psychology: Addresses the nature of the human will as a metaphysical question. James looks for a scientific theory of action to explain how humans come to exert their will. Will therefore is described as the lapse between the unconscious and the conscious.

_____. "What the Will Effects." In *Essays in Psychology*. Edited by Frederick Burkhardt. Cambridge, MA: Harvard University Press, 1983.

Psychology: This article describes the human will as the completion of a vision that is manifested in the unconscious of the individual. Human actions, therefore, are the coming together of the internal/unconscious vision and an external drive that pushes toward a realization of the vision.

Jones, Bessie W., and Vinson, Audrey. *The World of Toni Morrison: Explorations in Literary Criticism.* Dubuque, IA: Kendall Hunt Pub. Co., 1985.
   Literary criticism: A critique of the many works of Toni Morrison. A good resource for those wishing to understand how Morrison creates her interesting motifs and powerful characters through the use of symbolism. An added feature is an actual interview with Morrison.

Kung, Hans. *Does God Exist: An Answer for Today.* Translated by Edward Quinn. Garden City, NY: Doubleday, 1980.
   Theology: Kung offers a contemporary interpretation of free will in which God and humans work together. This interpretation, unlike earlier interpretations, accepts the notion of a God that is closely connected with human activity. God rather than being a distant, omnipotent force is a close, loving, and always forgiving Father.

Lanker, Brian. *I Dream a World.* New York: Stewart, Tabori, Chang, 1989.
   Photography, Biography: A wonderful book of photographs of Black women who have made a difference in this country. Each picture captures the character and strength of these women. A brief biographical sketch accompanies each photograph. In the introduction to the book Maya Angelou sums up what it means to be a strong willed Black woman.

Lerner, Gerda, ed. *Black Women in White America.* New York: Vintage Books, 1972.
   History, Sociology: A collection of writings written by Black women. Each woman speaks for herself and tells what it's like to be oppressed as a female and as a Black person. At the same time it offers hope because each of these women has survived. It is a book about the struggle for human dignity and how each woman, while victimized, emerged a winner.

Lincoln, C. Eric. *Race, Religion and the Continuing American Dilemma.* New York: Hill and Wang, 1984.
   Religion: Lincoln discusses how in the Black church Afrian Americans have come to understand God in a personal way that is not found in most human relationships and how this understanding has allowed African American people to participate in acts of freedom.

May, Rollo. *Love and Will.* New York: W. W. Norton, 1969.
   Psychology: Explores the notion that much of the apathy that is apparent in modern times is actually the absence of love and a lack of will. Thoroughly

examines the concepts of love and will and contains passages which reflect the research of Sigmund Freud and William James.

Mitchell, Henry. *Black Preaching.* San Francisco: Harper and Row, 1970, 1979.
    Theology: Characterizes the preaching tradition of the Black church. Mitchell discusses the natural ease in which the Black preacher uses hermeneutics to interpret the scripture to an appreciative congregation. The author believes that one reason the church has remained viable in the Black community is because Black preachers, through hermeneutical interpretation, have made religion relevant to their own experience.

Morrison, Toni. *Beloved.* New York: Alfred A. Knopf, 1974.
    Fiction: The story of Sethe, a woman who escaped slavery only to be haunted by the memory of a dead child. The story is of the unthinkable pain that Sethe has endured and the courage she exhibits as she struggles to keep the past from destroying her future.

_____. *The Bluest Eye.* New York: Washington Square Press, 1970.
    Fiction: A novel about a girl destroyed by racism and self hate. The story is told through the eyes of two little girls who are concerned for their friend, Pecola. The girls sympathize with Pecola who, because she is dark-skinned is considered ugly by her family and by a society that does not value her. The girls try to reclaim Pecola through their friendship, but it is too late. Pecola, victimized by her father and neglected by her mother, drifts further from reality.

_____. *Sula.* New York: New American Library, 1973.
    Fiction: The story of the friendship of two women, Sula Peace and Nel Wright. Both women are faced with profound choices which eventually drive them apart. The women suffer the consequences of their decisions, which is the loss of what is most important to both – each other.

Moynihan, Daniel P. *The Negro Family: The Case for National Action.* Washington, DC: U.S. Dept. of Labor, 1965.
    Social policy: A report on the crisis of the Black family. The report describes the Black family structure as patholgoical. This was based on the findings that a large number of Black families had female heads of household.

Nietzsche, Friedrich. *The Will to Power.* Edited by Walter Kaufmann. Translated by Walter Kaufmann and R. J. Hollingdale. New York: Vintage Books, 1967.
    Philosophy: A collection of Nietzsche's writings published after his death. Many passages in this work are devoted to reflections on the weakness of human beings. This weakness was seen as being the result of humankind's willingness to embody in God all that they should be claiming for themselves. Nietzsche believed that the ultimate goal for human beings was power, but we had been made to

believe that we must give up this power. The result of human weakness was nihilism, the complete breakdown of all known value systems.

Outhwaithe, William. "Hans Georg Gadamer." In *The Return of Grand Theory in the Human Sciences*, edited by Quentin Skinner, pp. 21–40. Cambridge, England: Cambridge University Press, 1985.
   Philosophy: Gives an explanation of the hermeneutic tradition of Hans George Gadamer. Gadamer wrote that understanding is derived only through a holistic process in which we move back and forth between specific parts of the text and our conception of it as a totality. An important component of hermeneutical interpretation is the process by which the investigator totally engages himself or herself with the text.

Polkinghorne, Donald. *Methodology for the Human Sciences*. Albany: State University of New York Press, 1983.
   Philosophy: An overview of developing methods of human science research. Describes their commonalities and variations and contains practical information on how to implement strategies in the field. It features sections on historical realism, systems and structures, phenomenology and hermeneutics.

Raines, Howell. *My Soul Is Rested*. New York: Penguin Books, 1977.
   African American history: A collection of interviews which tell the story of the Civil Rights Movement as seen by those who took a part in it. It tells of people who confronted hatred and violence with faith and courage. African American women included in this collection are Fannie Lou Hamer, Rosa Parks, Ruby Hurley, and Connie Curry.

Roderick, Rick. *Habermas and the Foundations of Critical Theory*. New York: St. Martin's Press, 1986.
   Sociology, Philosophy: Roderick explores the works of German theorist Jürgen Habermas. He presents two problems which appear and reappear throughout Habermas' work: the problem of developing a justification for the normative dimension of critical social theory and the problem of establishing a connection between theory and political practice.

Rychlak, Joseph. *Discovering Free Will and Personal Responsibility*. New York: Oxford University Press, 1979.
   Philosophy: Summarizes the debate on the existence and the nature of the human will from Aristotle and the early Greeks to the developing view of the early church.

St. Anselm. *Basic Writings*. Translated by S. N. Deane. LaSalle, IL: Open Court Pub. Co., 1962.
   Theology, Philosophy: Anselm writes about God as the First Cause or the

creator of all the universe. He uses the analogy of the artisan to explain how God could create something from nothing through His intention or will.

St. Augustine. *The Confessions of St. Augustine.* Westwood, NJ: Christian Library, 1984.
Theology, Philosophy: An expansion of the "deterministic thesis" of St. Paul in which the human will is equated with the fall of man. According to Augustine, free will is the cause of human suffering. It is only through denial of our wills and seeking God's will that human good is possible.

Schopenhauer, Arthur. Translated by Edward Quinn. *The World as Will and Idea.* Quoted in Hans Kung, *Does God Exist: An Answer for Today*, p. 359. Garden City, NY: Doubleday, 1980.
Theology, Philosophy: Presents the theory that all things are only the ideas of things. Things in and of themselves do not exist. Man can only experience himself in two ways: outwardly as object of the idea and inwardly as expression of will. The will to live is the innermost drive of human beings. Everything else exists because we will it to be.

Schutz, Alfred. Translated by George Walsh and Frederick Lehnert. *Phenomenology of the Social World.* Chicago: Northwestern University Press, 1967.
Philosophy: Using Husserlian phenomenology, Schutz provides a complete analysis of human action and its "intended meaning."

Smith, Kelly Miller. *Social Crisis Preaching.* Macon, GA: Mercer University Press, 1983.
Theology: Places hermeneutical interpretation within the context of the African American oral tradition. Hermeneutical interpretation in African American culture is appreciated as a gift and speakers are judged on their ability to "break down" a complicated idea or text.

Spellers, Hortense. "The Politics of Intimacy: A Discussion." In *Sturdy Black Bridges*, edited by Roseann Bell, Bettye Parker, and Beverly Guy-Sheftall, pp. 87–106. Garden City, NJ: Anchor Books, 1979.
Essay: Discusses the need for women to become their own historical subject. The author writes that Black women especially need to come to understand themselves and also define themselves to the rest of the world. The alternative is self destruction.

Spiegelburg, Herbert. *The Phenomenological Movement*, 3rd ed. The Hague: Martinus Nijhoff, 1982.
Philosophy: Outlines the seven steps to the phenomenological approach. These seven steps are guidelines which the researcher uses to conduct investigation.

The researcher has the liberty to eliminate some steps; the author suggests, however, that the first four steps are usually adhered to by most phenomenologists.

Stanage, Sherman. *Adult Education and Phenomenological Research*. Malabar, FL: Robert E. Krieger Pub. Co., 1987.

Adult education, Philosophy: Provides a rationale for adult educators to use phenomenology as a research methodology for the human sciences. One passage is devoted to a discussion of the process used to interpret a phenomenon. It suggests that the exploration of a phenomenon is an ongoing, open-ended process. This is especially true of human phenomena in the sense that a human being is not a static being, but always in the process of becoming.

Sterling, Dorothy, ed. *We are Your Sisters/Black Women in the Nineteenth Century*. New York: W. W. Norton, 1984.

History: This book portrays the lives of Black women before, during and after the Civil War through a well edited collection of letters, diary entries, memoirs, and the oral interviews of former slave women. This is a remarkable glimpse into the lives of these women who endured much in the struggle for freedom.

Thurman, Howard. *The Creative Encounter*. Richmond, IN: Friends United Press, 1972.

Religion: A passage which discusses the nature of the human spirit. The human spirit resists isolation and seeks to be connected with others as well as with a supreme being.

————. "Growing into Life." In *For the Inward Journey*, pp. 19–32. New York: Harcourt Brace Jovanovich, 1981.

Religion: A set of spiritual reflections which focus on the theme of spiritual growth development. As humans struggle to find the answers to the questions of life they find they must give up something for with knowledge comes the loss of innocence.

Walker, Alice. *The Color Purple*. New York: Harcourt Brace Jovanovich, 1982.

Fiction: A story about the power of friendship between two women. The central character, Celie, is a woman who has been abused by men. All she could do was survive. When her husband's lover, Shug Avery, comes to live with them, Celie's life changes. As the friendship between Celie and Shug grows, Celie transforms into a woman no longer afraid to demand what she wanted out of life.

————. *In Search of Our Mother's Gardens*. San Diego: Harcourt Brace Jovanovich, 1984.

Essays: Many of the essays in this book deal with the theme of the Black woman being somehow "suspended" in time. The Black woman survives by going inside herself and living in a state much like sleepwalking. On the surface the woman seems alive enough, but all true feeling is buried deep within.

_____. "Looking for Zora." In *I Love Myself When I Am Laughing and Then Again When I Am Looking Mean and Impressive,* edited by Alice Walker, pp. 297–313. New York: Feminist Press, 1979.

Essay: Alice Walker reminisces about her journey to Eatonville, Florida, the birthplace of Zora Neale Hurston. Walker visited the unmarked grave of Hurston in 1973 and erected a tombstone to honor her.

_____. *Meridian.* New York: Harcourt Brace Jovanovich, 1976.

Fiction: This novel is about Meridian, a powerful Black woman who risks everything for a cause she believes in. Meridian is not afraid to fight for what she wants, even if she has to fight alone. She is totally engaged in the struggle for civil rights and human dignity.

_____. *The Third Life of Grange Copeland.* New York: Harcourt Brace Jovanovich, 1970.

Fiction: The tragic story of a Black tenant farmer's growth into manhood. The novel portrays the violence which erupts between men and women when dreams are not realized.

Washington, Mary Helen. *Black Eyed Susans.* Garden City, NY: Anchor Books, 1975.

Fiction: An anthology of the works of Black female writers. The central theme for the works is Black women speaking out for themselves and sharing with the world their experiences. For the first time Black females were being asked to write their own history.

_____. "An Interview with Alice Walker." In *Sturdy Black Bridges,* edited by Roseann Bell, Bettye Parker, and Beverly Guy-Sheftall, pp. 133–149. Garden City, NY: Anchor Books, 1975.

Interview: In this interview Alice Walker speaks about the evolution of her characters. She considers how the lives of Black women have changed as a result of the Civil Rights Movement of the sixties and how her characters will reflect these changes.

_____. *Midnight Birds.* Garden City, NY: Anchor Books, 1980.

Fiction: An anthology of the writings of contemporary Black women writers. This collection includes works by Alice Walker, Paulette Childress White, Ntozake Shange, Alexis Deveaux, Toni Morrison, and Toni Cade Bambara. A central theme is the Black woman's struggle to forge an identity larger than the one society would place on them.

White, Joseph. *The Psychology of Blacks: An Afro-American Perspective.* Engelwood Cliffs, NJ: Prentice-Hall, 1984.

Psychology: Offers a perspective on the psyche of African Americans.

Community and relationship are considered essential to survival in an environment that is often painful and tragic. Part of the survival equipment of the African American is the ability to face misfortune with a smile; to laugh when one would rather cry; to push forward and endure.

Winger, Ernst, ed. *Discourse in Free Will*. New York: Frederick Unger Publishers, 1974.
    Religion: A translation of the basic texts of Martin Luther and Erasmus. These writings reveal the characteristic differences in the early Catholic and Protestant positions concerning human nature and the question of the freedom of will.

Woodson, Carter G. *The Mis-Education of the Negro*. Washington, DC: Associated Publishers, 1933; reprint ed., Trenton, NJ: Africa World Press, Inc., 1990.
    Education: Written as a comment on the education of African Americans in 1933, but it could have been written in 1990. The author contends that until African Americans determine their own educational needs, based upon their reality, they will continue to be controlled. This book is a book about self-reliance and self-determination.

Wright, Jeremiah. Sermon, *Evolution vs. Creation*. Trinity United Church of Christ, Chicago, 9 March 1988.
    Sermon: A discussion about the theory of evolution versus the theory of creation. According to this pastor one does not have to choose one or the other. The two theories are not in conflict with one another because they answer two different questions. The theory of evolution tells us what happened, but the theory of creation tells us who was responsible. The belief in God as Creator is central to the Black church and it stems from traditional African religion, which fully recognizes the existence of a superior being.

Index